Classic **Fel**

Morning mist clears on the way to Crinkle Crags with Pike o' Blisco in the distance (route 18)

Classic Fell Walks in the
Lake District

Carl Rogers

www.lakeland-fellwalking.co.uk

MARA BOOKS

www.marabooks.co.uk
www.northerneyebooks.com

First published in April 2011 by **Mara Books**,
22 Crosland Terrace, Helsby, Frodsham, Cheshire WA6 9LY.

Telephone: 01928 723744

ISBN 978-1-902512-24-2

Advice to readers and users of this guide

Whilst every effort has been made to ensure that the information in this book is correct, the author or the publisher can accept no responsibility for errors, loss or injury however caused. Check all details before you proceed. Your use of this book indicates your assumption of the risks involved in mountain walking and scrambling and is an acknowledgement of your own sole responsibility for your safety.

Fix the Fells

It is estimated that seven million pairs of boots hit the trails of Lakeland every year, the wear, exacerbated by the ravages of the wild upland weather, causes ugly erosion to develop. Hence I would urge you to match your achievement with a sense of custodial care by visiting **www.fixthefells.co.uk** and help secure this remarkable mountain landscape for those who follow you.

Layout and design by Carl Rogers, Mara Books 2011

Text and photographs © Carl Rogers 2011, except front and back covers, and pages 74 and 84 © Stewart Smith 2011 (www.stewartsmithphotography.co.uk)

Contents

Introduction

THE LAKE DISTRICT is probably the best known walking area in the British Isles and whether you are lover of high places or a low-level stroller, you will find plenty in this beautiful corner of England to entertain you with woodlands, lakes, tarns, fells and mountains in abundance. The Lake District has captivated visitors for two centuries or more inspiring many of our greatest artists and providing countless individuals with their first taste of adventure and exploration which has remained with them for the rest of their lives.

The Lakeland fells were made famous (or at least brought to the attention of the vast majority) by the late Alfred Wainwright who began his unique series of pictorial guidebooks over half a century ago. His

Grasmoor from Crummock Water

Scafell and Yewbarrow seen form Looking Stead (Mosedale Horseshoe)

beautiful hand-drawn books list over 214 fells (many of them obscure when he began his exploration) and outline just about every route of ascent on each fell. This could be said to have opened up the Lakeland fells in much the same way as Hugh Munro's listing of Scotland's 3,000-foot 'Munros' did for the Scottish mountains.

Today 'doing the Wainwrights' is a growing obsession for many, but it is a big undertaking. Completing all 214 fells on Wainwright's list will take the average walker, with limited time, many years to complete. With that in mind this book has been compiled as an introduction to the Lakeland fells and pulls together what are generally considered to be the classic full-day fell walking rounds—a Lakeland 'must do' list.

But what is a 'classic' and who decides such things? I suppose this is very much down to the individual and everyone who walks in the Lakeland fells will develop their own collection of favourites, but I found that when I sat down to decide what would be included in this guide I was surprised at how similar my own list was with just about everyone I asked and almost every book I opened. Even Wainwright himself agreed. There are some differences of course, but I am confident that

Evening shadows on Grasmoor

the walks in the following pages represent not just what I consider to be the best that the Lake District has to offer, but can confidently be called 'Classics'. These are, and will continue to be, Lakeland's classic fell walking rounds.

If you are new to the Lakeland fells, or are just starting out on your round of the Wainwrights, then surely the classic rounds are the place to begin. By time you have completed the twenty routes in this book you will not only have all the big names under your belt, you will also have climbed all the four highest fells which rise above 3,000 feet, as well as over a third of the summits on Wainwright's list—78 in total.

A note of caution (what this guide won't do)—although all the routes in the following pages carry a detailed route description, I have assumed that anyone following them will have the ability to navigate independently of the book using a large scale Ordnance Survey map and compass. (The Ordnance Survey 1:25,000 Explorer map sheets OL4, 5, 6 and 7 cover all the walks in this book.) This is not an optional skill, it is a basic requirement and without it you are not safe to either walk or scramble on the fells. It is important to remember that this book is merely a guide to a selection of *possible* routes. They are not the *only* routes and the book will not help you if you wander off the suggested route and become lost, particularly in bad weather or poor visibility.

It should also be noted that although the photographs which illustrate the guide were taken throughout the year, including full winter conditions, **all the routes are intended as summer walks or scrambles in fine, dry conditions**. Poor visibility, wind, rain and especially winter conditions with ice and snow, turn the fells and mountains into a very different environment. If you venture onto the fells in these conditions, be sure you are equipped and experienced enough to deal with them. For winter walking in snow and ice conditions, an ice axe and the knowledge of how to use it is a minimum requirement. Suitable clothing is just as essential.

On the routes labelled **SCRAMBLE** you will need to be confident climbing over rocks which, although not technically difficult (not graded rock climbs), will still require agility, a steady head and could well be in an exposed position where a fall would be serious. Having said that, the scrambles described are generally completed without the use of ropes and specialist equipment in normal conditions, ie. dry, summer weather with good visibility and free from snow and ice. If you are in any doubt about the above, avoid these routes until you have more experience. Remember, all the scrambles become winter climbs under ice and snow and are beyond the scope of this guide.

Looking over the shoulder of Fleetwith Pike to Great Gable and Kirk Fell

List of Wainwrights covered by this book in descending altitude

Summit	Section	Height	Route
Scafell Pike	*The West*	978m/3,209ft	8
Scafell	*The West*	964m/3,163ft	9
Helvellyn	*The East*	950m/3,117ft	12
Skiddaw	*The North*	931m/3,054ft	2
Great End	*The West*	910m/2,986ft	8
Bowfell	*The South*	902m/2,959ft	(18), 19
Great Gable	*The West*	899m/2,949ft	11
Pillar	*The West*	892m/2,920ft	10
Catstycam	*The East*	890m/3,156ft	12
Esk Pike	*The South*	885m/2,904ft	19
Fairfield	*The East/South*	873m/2,864ft	13, 16
Blencathra	*The North*	868m/2,848ft	1
Crinkle Crags	*The South*	859m/2,818ft	18
Grasmoor	*The North*	852m/2,795ft	(3), 5
St Sunday Crag	*The East*	841m/2,759ft	13
Scoat Fell	*The West*	841m/2,759ft	10
Crag Hill (Eel Crag)	*The North*	839m/2,753ft	3
High Street	*The East/South*	828m/2,717ft	14, 15
Red Pike (Wasdale)	*The West*	826m/2,710ft	10
Hart Crag	*The South*	822m/2,697ft	13, 16
Steeple	*The West*	819m/2,687ft	10
Lingmell	*The West*	807m/2,648ft	8
High Stile	*The West*	806m/2,644ft	6
Old Man of Coniston	*The South*	803m/2,635ft	20
Kirk Fell	*The West*	802m/2,631ft	11
Swirl How	*The South*	802m/2,631ft	20
Green Gable	*The West*	801m/2,628ft	11
Brim Fell	*The South*	796m/2,612ft	20
Dove Crag	*The South*	792m/2,598ft	16
Rampsgill Head	*The East*	792m/2,598ft	14
Grisedale Pike	*The North*	791m/2,595ft	3
Thornthwaite Crag	*The South*	784m/2,572ft	15
Great Carrs	*The South*	780m/2,559ft	20
Kidsty Pike	*The East*	780m/2,559ft	14
Harter Fell	*The East/South*	778m/2,552ft	14, 15
Dow Crag	*The South*	778m/2,552ft	20
Grey Friar	*The South*	773m/2,536ft	20
Sail	*The North*	773m/2,536ft	3
Wandope	*The North*	772m/2,533ft	(3), 5
Hopegill Head	*The North*	770m/2,526ft	5
Great Rigg	*The South*	766m/2,513ft	16
Mardale Ill Bell	*The East/South*	760m/2,493ft	14, 15
Ill Bell	*The South*	757m/2,484ft	15

Red Pike (Buttermere)	*The West*	755m/2,477ft	6
Slight Side	*The West*	748m/2,454ft	9
Carl Side	*The North*	746m/2,448ft	2
High Crag	*The West*	744m/2,441ft	6
Robinson	*The North*	737m/2,418ft	4
Harrison Stickle	*The South*	736m/2,415ft	17
Long Side	*The North*	734m/2,408ft	2
Kentmere Pike	*The South*	730m/2,395ft	15
Hindscarth	*The North*	727m/2,385ft	4
Thunacar Knotts	*The South*	723m/2,372ft	17
Foswick	*The South*	720m/2,362ft	15
Pike o' Stickle	*The South*	709m/2,326ft	17
Whiteside	*The North*	707m/2,320ft	5
Yoke	*The South*	706m/2,316ft	15
Pike o' Blisco	*The South*	705m/2,313ft	18
Pavey Ark	*The South*	699m/2,298ft	17
Ullock Pike	*The North*	690m/2,264ft	2
Loft Crag	*The South*	680m/2,231ft	16
Scar Crags	*The North*	672m/2,205ft	(3)
Whiteless Pike	*The North*	660m/2,165ft	5
High Pike	*The South*	656m/2,152ft	16
Fleetwith Pike	*The West*	648m/2,126ft	7
Rossett Pike	*The South*	648m/2,126ft	19
Causey Pike	*The North*	637m/2,090ft	(3)
Yewbarrow	*The West*	627m/2,057ft	10
Birks	*The East*	622m/2,041ft	(13)
Heron Pike	*The South*	612m/2,008ft	16
Haystacks	*The West*	597m/1,959ft	7
Hartsop Above How	*The East*	579m/1,900ft	13
Shipman Knotts	*The South*	587m/1,926ft	15
Outerside	*The North*	568m/1,864ft	(3)
Low Pike	*The South*	508m/1,667ft	16
Barrow	*The North*	455m/1,493ft	(3)
Nab Scar	*The South*	449m/1,473ft	16
Rannerdale Knotts	*The North*	355m/1,165ft	5

Leaving the summit of Pike o' Blisco with Bowfell behind (route 18)

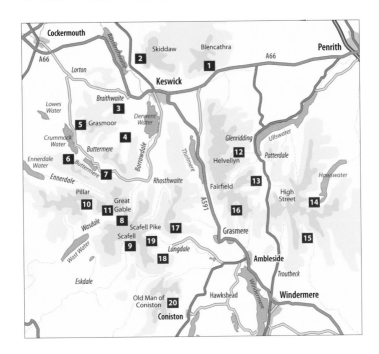

Useful information

A full list of the Wainwrights along with information on each summit is available on Wikipedia (www.wikipedia.org).

Weather forecasts

www.mwis.org.uk/
www.bbc.co.uk/weather
www.metoffice.gov.uk

Webcams

There is nothing quite like seeing how things are right now. Live webcams enable you to do just that. At the time of writing one of the best sites for live webcams is: www.5hort5.co.uk/webcams.html

In case of emergency dial 999 or 112 and ask for the Cumbria police, and then for Mountain Rescue.

The North

Hall's Fell ridge, Blencathra

Blencathra showing both Sharp Edge (R) and Hall's Fell ridge (L)

1. Blencathra by Sharp Edge & Hall's Fell ridge

Outline: SCRAMBLE *Initially steep walking on good footpaths leads over the broad grassy ridge of Scales Fell and beside the upper River Glenderamakin to reach the sheltered hollow containing Scales Tarn directly below Sharp Edge. Exposed scrambling on Sharp Edge takes you directly onto the summit plateau. Descent is by the easier but still rocky edge of Hall's Fell ridge which takes a direct and spectacular 600 metre line down the mountain's southern face.*

Distance: *9km/5½ miles.*

Height gained: *800m/2,615ft.*

Summits: *Blencathra (sometimes known as 'Saddleback').*

Starting point: *Limited parking is available in a layby on the A66 at Scales (grid ref: NY 344 269). Alternatively there is a small parking area along the minor lane about 700m beyond the 'White Horse Inn' at Scales. Park immediately after the little bridge. Grid ref: NY 349 272.*

Bʟᴇɴᴄᴀᴛʜʀᴀ ɪs ᴛʜᴇ ɢʀᴇᴀᴛ ᴍᴏᴜɴᴛᴀɪɴ ʙᴜʟᴋ which greets the motorist entering the Lake District from the northeast along the A66. And what a greeting—no gentle introductions, this mountain hits you like a fist and reveals all in a magnificent medley of ridges and buttresses.

The main routes on the mountain use easy access points on the A66 including this classic round via Sharp Edge and Hall's Fell ridge. Sharp Edge is is one of the best low-end scrambles in the Lake District and takes a direct line up a narrow rock ridge. The scrambling is straightforward but exposed, requiring care and may not be to everyone's liking. If you enjoy Sharp Edge however, Hall's Fell ridge provides the logical descent being easier and less exposed, but still providing interesting scrambling. Options avoiding Sharp Edge also are included.

The route: From the parking area walk back along the lane and take the signed footpath on the right in about 100m. (If you parked down

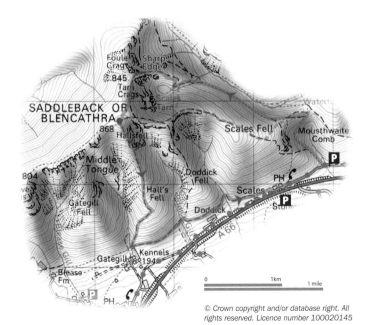

on the main road, reach this point by following the lane from the 'White Horse Inn' and just before it bends left down to cross the stream the signed path is on the left.) The path is well used and obvious and heads up the left-hand side of the little valley of Mousthwaite Comb, before swinging diagonally-right across the steep valley head to the broad saddle on the skyline.

The saddle is a good place to take a breather and survey the route ahead. Sharp Edge can be seen rising impressively above the upper valley of the River Glenderamakin with the rounded, grassy shoulder of Scales Fell to the left. Southwards the view opens out across the moors and woods of Threlkeld Common to the rolling crests of the Dodds.

The path swings left now along the broad grassy saddle towards Scales Fell and in about 400m forks. The path ahead continues up the broad, gentle slopes of Scales Fell along the edge of the steep, rocky southern face of the mountain to reach the summit. *If you have doubts about Sharp Edge, this is a straightforward route to the summit.*

For Sharp Edge bear right at the fork and follow the path which takes a contouring line up the valley towards the pass on the skyline separating Blencathra from Bannerdale Crags with the beck down to the right. About halfway up the valley the path crosses the stream which cascades out of the unseen combe above. Cross the stream here, then bear left up the pitched path which makes the short steep climb beside the beck to Scales Tarn, cradled in an impressive mountain hollow, its headwall rising 200m above the tarn.

Two walkers begin Sharp Edge seen from Scales Tarn

Scramblers on Sharp Edge seen from Tarn Crags

Over 150m above the tarn, Sharp Edge strikes an impressive skyline fringed by broken rock slabs and steep screes. It looks harder and more exposed than it is and many have second thoughts here. On a busy day parties separate by the tarn—those intent on the ridge head right up the steep approach path, the rest keep left up the rounded back of Scales Fell.

Take the footpath up to the start of the ridge. Scrambling is easy at first and begins up a 'V' shaped groove to reach the narrow crest *(there is a lower path immediately before this which traverses below the ridge crest on the right-hand side avoiding much of the best scrambling, but still joining the main route just before the crux)*.

The ridge crest is quite narrow and there is exposure on both sides, but the scrambling is straightforward and much of it can be walked with just the occasional steadying hand if you feel confident enough. The central section resembles a rock pavement but the polished rock can be slippery in the wet. The crux comes just before the ridge joins the main bulk of the mountain where some small pinnacles must be passed. The easiest line bypasses them on the right by means of a sloping ledge which some may find intimidating on account of the drop into a gully on the right. This can be slippy in the wet. The alternative is by delicate moves over a considerable drop on the left-hand side of the crest. (The lower path which avoids the crest joins just before this so you can't avoid these crux moves.)

This leads to a gap in the ridge before the final slabby rocks which lead up onto the summit. These can be tackled direct by delicate climbing on good rock, or a slightly easier line can be taken up a shallow gully just to the right of centre. The scrambling ends almost on the summit plateau where a good path heads left along the top of Tarn Crags to the summit.

The view from here is superb—especially south down the 600m south face of the mountain to the A66 and the greenery of Saint John's in the Vale. Just about every Lakeland fell of note is visible, from the Coniston Fells beyond Thirlmere, past Bowfell, Esk Pike, Scafell Pike, Great Gable, the Buttermere and Derwent Fells, to the neighbouring giant of Skiddaw.

The out-and-back walk along the ridge to Gategill Fell is recommended before you consider the descent. *The easiest descent is by the broad, gentle ridge of Scales Fell, a well-used route on the obvious path which heads due east to join the outward route on the saddle*

Looking back up Hall's Fell ridge from just below the rocky section

Blencathra and Hall's Fell ridge seen in profile from the A66

above Mousthwaite Comb. If Sharp Edge has whetted your appetite for scrambling, the 600m long Hall's Fell ridge makes the perfect descent. This is much easier and more straightforward than Sharp Edge and has little if any of the latter's exposure. It is also easy to locate, even in poor visibility, as it falls directly from the summit cairn. The upper half of the ridge contains almost all of the scrambling which can be varied at will or even avoided altogether by paths mainly to the left of the crest.

The lower section of the ridge is steep rather than rocky, the path trending right to reach the stream of Gate Gill with walled fields ahead and a small wood. Don't cross the stream here, turn sharp left and follow the good footpath parallel to the wall on the right. After you cross the next stream (Doddick Gill), you will need to make an unexpected (and unwelcome) rise around the walled fields ahead to continue. The final obstacle is a short scramble down a rock step to cross Scaley Beck. About 400m further on take the path right between cottages to reach the main road where a left turn will take you back to the 'White Horse Inn' to complete the route.

Skiddaw and Ullock Pike from Bassenthwaite Lake

2. *Skiddaw by Ullock Pike*

Outline: *After a leisurely start in the conifer plantations of Dodd Wood a climb is made onto the excellent ridge leading up over Ullock Pike with superb views. This is followed to the final summit slopes—a steep climb over scree. Descent is steep and direct over Carl Side with a return along woodland trails.*

Distance: *10.74km/6½ miles.*

Height gained: *955m/3,130ft.*

Summits: *Ullock Pike, Long Side, Carl Side, Skiddaw.*

Starting point: *There is a small car park at the Old Sawmills Tearooms in Dodd Wood. This lies on the A591 about 5km/3 miles north of Keswick. Grid ref: NY 235 281.*

SKIDDAW IS MOST FAMOUSLY SEEN as an impressive backdrop to pictur-esque views of Derwent Water and its surrounding fells. It is also hard to avoid its imposing bulk from the narrow streets of Keswick, the town which nestles at its feet. It was probably this prominence, along with the ease with which it can be ascended which has drawn the crowds since Victorian times when visitors could hire guides to take them to the summit for the magnificent view. Not much has changed, Skiddaw is one of the most popular summits in the Lake District and there is little doubt that it has one of the best views.

The main problem with an ascent of Skiddaw is finding an interesting route. Its geology has given it a uniformity broken by few crags or ridges, its upper slopes a mix of shale and grass. Only to the northwest does the mountain show any form where it throws down a long sweeping ridge towards Bassenthwaite Lake. This ridge can be used as an excellent route to the summit with a low-level link through Dodd Wood to return.

The route: From the car park take the signed 'All Trails' path over the wooden footbridge and turn sharp left almost immediately onto the footpath which heads down beside the stream towards the road, then curves rightwards up to a forest road. Take the path opposite and a little to the right. This path heads leftwards rising gently.

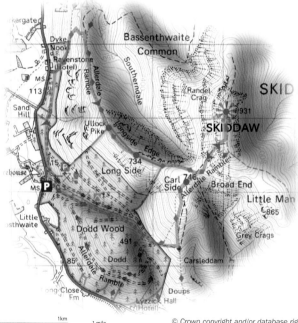

Looking back to Long Side and Ullock Pike

Where the path levels, ignore a path on the right by a small rock face, continuing ahead on the contouring path. After a wooden footbridge the forest path begins to descend. Shortly there is a fork—bear right here climbing again, soon emerging from the dense pines to a broad view out over Bassenthwaite Lake. Continue on the contouring path to meet a track coming up from the left. Turn right along this and in about 50m bear right on a path which leads up to a gate onto the open fell.

A good footpath rises diagonally leftwards beside the fence. Where the path forks, bear right away from the fence and climb to reach the crest of the rounded ridge on the skyline.

Almost on the ridge crest you meet the main ridge path at a T junction. Turn right here and soon you will get your first glimpse of the route ahead in the form of Skiddaw's great, grey bulk rising at the head of Southerndale. The route up the ridge to Ullock Pike is well-defined and you now have the advantage of good views all around. The ancient slates from which Skiddaw is formed mean that crags and outcrops are rare and generally the mountain lacks any detailed interest. This ridge is the exception, its narrow crest is a delight and as you climb grand views open out on both sides.

Although Ullock Pike appears as a distinct and quite shapely fell from Bassenthwaite Lake, you will discover that its summit is little more than a slight rise on Carl Side's long north ridge. Once you are on its summit however, you can add views south to Keswick, Derwent Water and the distant mass of Helvellyn and Fairfield to the growing panorama.

After Ullock Pike the easy gradient allows you to cruise along the ridge to Long Side and then on a traversing path which cuts out the unnecessary diversion to Carl Side (this will be visited on the descent) to the broad saddle which joins Carl Side to the main bulk of the mountain. There is a tiny pool here, Carlside Tarn (a useful landmark in poor visibility), and the main path can be seen climbing diagonally-leftwards (northeast) up the shattered hillside to the summit ridge, a climb of about 200m.

Once over this section the steep, shaly slopes fall back to the broad summit plateau and you are greeted by views east across the wild moors known as 'Back o' Skidda' to Blencathra with the northern Pennines in the distance beyond Penrith. The highest point is at the northern end where there is a small stone wind shelter.

Standing well back from the surrounding fells, Skiddaw enjoys wide views in every direction. In clear conditions the view north is across the Solway Firth to Dumfrieshire and the Scottish lowlands, east it takes in the hidden moors of the Skiddaw Forest and out over the northern

Skiddaw, Carl Side and the distant Little Man seen from Long Side

Pennines. South and west you have most of the Lakeland fells arranged in a great arc centred on Keswick and Derwent Water.

To return, retrace your steps back to Carlside Tarn on the saddle separating Skiddaw from Carl Side and take the path ahead over the rounded, poorly-defined summit of Carl Side. Again the views are superb and you will now have the town of Keswick and Derwent Water spread out before you like a map. The path soon steepens heading almost due south with Derwent Water directly ahead.

Continue the descent until you reach an area of prominent white rocks (marked as 'White Stones' on the Ordnance Survey map). These are obvious and are almost the only rocks you will encounter on this descent. Take the traversing path which heads right here. In about 100m or so there is a small cairn and a rough but visible path on the left. Turn left and follow this path as it heads diagonally down to meet a forest road visible below crossing the gap between Carl Side and the attractive little summit of Dodd.

Cross the stile leading onto the road and turn right. As you begin to descend there is a fork—keep left here. Follow this unsurfaced forest road for about 1km/¾ mile, ignoring two tracks which rise to the left. About 150m after the second track, take the path which forks right down through the woods to a crossing path. Turn right and follow this path back to the car park to complete the route.

The view south from Carl Side to Keswick and Derwent Water

Grisedale Pike, Eel Crag and Outerside near the end of the walk

3. The Coledale Horseshoe

Outline: *A long but gradual ascent of Grisedale Pike's east ridge leads to the first high summit of the day. This is followed by straightforward walking along the ridge to Hopegill Head and Sand Hill before the descent to Coledale Hause. A steady climb from the hause to Eel Crag is the last great effort of the day. Easy walking along the fine elevated ridge to Sail is followed by the descent to High Moss. A series of optional minor tops and a gradual descent back to Braithwaite.*

Distance: *15km/9½ miles.*

Height gained: *1,300m/4,270ft.*

Summits: *Grisedale Pike, Hopegill Head, Eel Crag (Crag Hill), Sail (Grasmoor, Wandhope, Scar Crags, Causey Pike, Outerside & Barrow optional).*

Starting point: *The village of Braithwaite, near Keswick. There are no official car parks making parking difficult. The best options are in a small parking area at the start of the Whinlatter Pass or on a loop of the old road opposite the village on the A66.*
Grid ref: NY 237 236.

Heading for Grisedale Pike at the start of the Coledale Horseshoe in perfect winter conditions

ONE OF THE MOST POPULAR and impressive viewpoints in the Lake District is the modest summit of Latrigg which stands directly above the town of Keswick, knee high to the bulk of Skiddaw. From its broad grassy summit you look out across Keswick and Derwent Water to the distant Scafell group beyond Borrowdale, and east to the rounded backs of Helvellyn and the Dodds. But the real attention grabber is the view west to the mass of sweeping ridges which make up the Derwent Fells. Their sedimentary bedrock forms few crags, but has instead weathered into a series of soft ridges; steep but primarily grassy. Seen as a group they have the appearance of wave crests about to break against each other. Perfect fell walking terrain.

There are a number of superb rounds in these fells, but the classic is the circuit of Coledale taking in the highest and most well known summits in the group—Grisedale Pike and Eel Crag.

The route: Follow the Whinlatter Pass road out of Braithwaite passing the 'Royal Oak' pub. Soon the lane swings right and begins to climb. At a track access with small parking area on the left, take the signed path for Grisedale Pike which rises rightwards up steps. This climbs diagonally up the slope soon giving wide views across the valley to the bulky western slopes of Skiddaw.

The path swings left shortly and rises up onto the rounded ridge of Kinn where you will get your first real view of the route ahead to Grisedale Pike with the valley of Coledale down to your left. The Coledale Horseshoe follows the skyline ahead of you, from Grisedale Pike to the pass of Coledale Hause and up to Eel Crag—the high point of the day—then along the ridge to Sail and Outerside which can be seen across Coledale.

The path ahead is straightforward and after a slight dip on the broad ridge, makes a steady rise to Sleet How, where you will be able to enjoy a close-up view of the final, steep section of Grisedale Pike's east ridge. There is a small amount of slaty rock higher up giving the summit the feel of a true mountain.

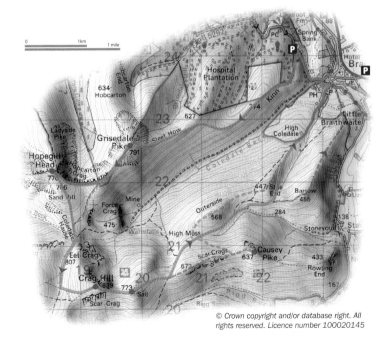

Grisedale Pike and Coledale showing the approach ridge over Kinn

In clear conditions the view from the summit is excellent and is dominated by the bulk of Skiddaw rising across the broad, low-lying vale of the River Derwent and the high tops of the Derwent Fells, especially the shapely, pointed summit of Hopegill Head along the ridge to the west.

From Grisedale Pike the path continues west along the ridge crest towards Hopegill Head. After a subsidiary top, unnamed on the Ordnance Survey map, the path forks. *The shortest and easiest option is to follow the path ahead which swings left to Coledale Hause, the broad saddle separating Coledale from Gasgale Gill.* If you want to include Hopegill Head and Sand Hill bear right here and follow the path along the edge of the impressive Hobcarton Crag.

Hopegill Head is a striking summit perched on the very brink of Hobcarton Crag, a sight which will have enticed you all the way from Grisedale Pike. To the west the ridge narrows to form the appealing crest of Whiteside, its steep, shattered south face falling over 300m to Gasgale Gill. *The mountain's north ridge swings more gracefully to Ladyside Pike, a short out-and-back walk for the summit bagger.*

To continue, take the well-worn path which heads southeast over the indistinct top of Sand Hill, shards of slate underfoot rather than sand. A steeper descent brings you to Coledale Hause, where several paths converge.

(If time or inclement weather is pressing, you can shorten the walk here by taking the path left into Pudding Beck hollow to join the mining road which can be followed back to Braithwaite.)

To continue, follow the path ahead which rises steadily to the broad saddle separating Grasmoor from Eel Crag. *At the path T junction you have the option to add Grasmoor to your summit count by an out-and-back walk to the right of just over 2km/1¼ miles.*

Take the path left now and rise to the broad, featureless summit of Eel Crag. *The summit of Wandhope—a short detour over to the right just before Eel Crag—is a superb viewpoint with panoramas down the steep sweeping, 'V'-shaped valley of Sail Beck to Buttermere, the fin-like crest of Ard Crags and the Newands Pass.*

Eel Crag (Crag Hill on the OS map) is the high point of the walk at 838m/2,753ft and probably gives the best view of all—from Skiddaw and Blencathra past the Dodds, Helvellyn and Fairfield to the Langdale Pikes and almost all the central fells around Scafell Pike. Nearer at hand lie the ridges of the Derwent Fells, laid out like the hedges in a

The stunning view of Skiddaw from Barrow near the end of the walk

maze, with the High Stile range beyond. Out across the sea to the west, you should be able to see the Isle of Man with the Scottish Lowlands beyond the Solway Firth.

From Eel Crag follow the path almost due east down the narrowing ridge before a short rise to the summit of Sail and then on to the next saddle known as Sail Pass.

If you are collecting summits it is easy to tick off Scar Crags and Causey Pike by continuing along the ridge ahead. If you do this return along the ridge after Causey Pike and take the diagonal path which drops right (north) between Scar Crags and Causey Pike. This takes you to the plateau of High Moss immediately north of Scar Crags.

High Moss is reached more easily by taking the path left (north) from Sail Pass and heading diagonally down the northern slopes of Scar Crags.

High Moss sits at the head of Stonycroft Gill which separates Causey Pike from the Outerside–Barrow ridge. A good path descends from here above the beck and across the southern slopes of Outerside to eventually reach the Newlands road at Stonycroft. For the easiest option follow this path, but bear left as it begins to descend to Barrow Door, the gap between the little summits of Stile End and Barrow. From here a straightforward path heads northeast (left) to join a lane above Braithwaite. Follow this lane back to Braithwaite to complete the walk.

If you have the energy, the minor summits of Outerside, Stile End and Barrow make a fine end to this ridge walk. Start with Outerside by bearing left off the main path shortly after High Moss. The ridge is easy to follow over Outerside, Stile End and finally Barrow. Follow Barrow's well-defined northeast ridge with a grand view ahead to Skiddaw. At the bottom of the ridge bear left and follow the right of way through a farm (Braithwaite Lodge) to join the farm access road. Follow the farm road back to Braithwaite.

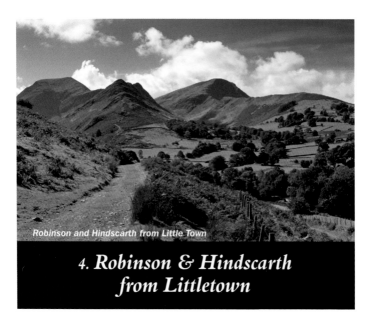

Robinson and Hindscarth from Little Town

4. *Robinson & Hindscarth from Littletown*

Outline: *Starting in the narrow lanes of the Newlands Valley the route climbs by a farm road onto a narrow grass edge with wide views. A little easy scrambling leads onto the upper fell to reach Robinson's broad summit with its wide views. Straightforward easy-angled walking on the connecting ridge leads to the neighbouring summit of Hindscarth. Descent is by the long northeast ridge which will take you gently back to the valley.*

Distance: *10.5km/6½ miles.*

Height gained: *790m/2,590ft.*

Summits: *Robinson, Hindscarth.*

Starting point: *There is limited parking in a layby in the lane which leads from the hamlet of Little Town to the Newlands Pass road immediately south of the bridge over Keskadale Beck.*
Grid ref: NY 232 194.

THE SIGHT OF ROBINSON AND HINDSCARTH'S graceful, grassy edges rising from the folds of the Newlands Valley is surely one of the most appealing skylines in the Lake District. These two fells are just about high enough and rough enough to feel like mountains, yet their soft contours glide underfoot with a reassuring ease. Only at one point in this classic round will the average walker be tested to any degree, where Robinson's northeast ridge narrows near Blea Crags. Two minutes of easy scrambling and you can move back into cruise mode for the rest of the walk.

Views in clear conditions are superb from this central location, with just about every group of fells visible.

Looking back along High Snab Bank from the shoulder of Robinson

The route: From the lane turn along the signed no through road to 'Newlands Ch ¼'. This leads to the church and a handful of farms. Pass the little church and continue along the gently rising lane to pass 'High Snab' farm. The lane continues ahead, the tarmac ending beyond 'Low High Snab' farm. Keep ahead again, now on a walled farm track to reach the open fell after a large gate. A little further on turn sharp right on a path which heads steeply and directly up through the bracken to gain the grassy ridge crest passing a group of pines on the right. This is the first real climb and as you reach the ridge crest you get a hint of the views to come as you look rightwards down the Newlands Valley to Little Town with an unfamiliar side-on view of Catbells rising behind.

The walk along the grassy edge of High Snab Bank with its superb views into Keskadale and over to Eel Crag, Sail and Causey Pike, is easy-angled and enables you to catch your breath for the final climb to Robinson rising impressively ahead. A short dip at the end of the ridge followed by one or two rock steps—which although easy will require the use of both hands and feet—lead onto the high shoulder of the mountain, the path running close to the edge of Robinson Crags on the right. This broken face sweeps impressively into the wild depths of Keskadale.

You will feel that that you have reached the summit many times before you actually stand beside the highest point as each cairned rise ahead gives way to one more. Surprisingly, the summit is a broad plateau large enough for a game of cricket, the highest point marked by a small stone wind shelter rather than just a cairn. This unremarkable setting is none-the-less a superb viewpoint, the high central fells more than likely grabbing your attention in clear conditions. Great Gable is the dominant fell with Scafell Pike to the left and Scafell to the right. The Grasmoor group to the north also looks superb from here.

A good footpath heads almost due south across the plateau to meet a fence where it turns left. Follow this path, descending beside the fence along the broad ridge forming the divide between Little Dale and the unseen depths of Buttermere to the right. Frustratingly the lake remains hidden all the way to Hindscarth, the eye drawn instead by the dark bulk of Fleetwith Pike seen in profile across the Honister Pass.

At the low point on the ridge the path forks. The path ahead is steep and leads along the ridge to Dalehead, the path left heads diagonally across the fell to Hinscarth. Take the latter path and in ten minutes

Easy walking along High Snab Bank with Robinson rising ahead

Looking across Scope Beck to High Snab Bank and Robinson from Scope End

or so you will be standing beside Hindscarth's summit cairn—almost a carbon copy of its twin across the hollow of Little Dale. The main difference in the view from here is that it is more dominated by the ridge from Dalehead to High Spy and Maiden Moor.

Head north to a second stone windshelter where the descent ridge comes into view below. The path is easily followed down through broken rocks before the lower grass and heather of Scope End is reached.

This ridge is similar to High Snab Bank in the rise to Robinson and is almost as easy underfoot. The view to the valley below and across the Newlands Valley to Causey Pike, Sail and Eel Crag is superb. Robinson, rising at the head of High Snab Bank, also presents an impressive sight.

At the end of the ridge, descend more steeply to reach a footpath T junction. Turn right here and walk down past mining spoil to reach a farm track near Low Snab Farm. Turn left through the gate to follow a permissive path past the farmhouse and along the access road. At the Newlands Church, turn right and follow the lane back to the layby to complete the route.

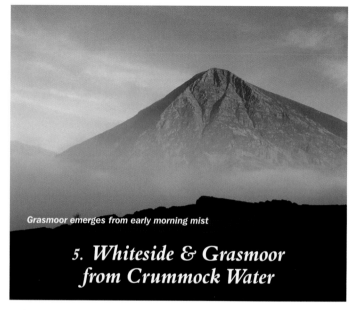

Grasmoor emerges from early morning mist

5. *Whiteside & Grasmoor from Crummock Water*

Outline: *A steep climb from Lanthwaite Green to the fine edge of Whiteside and Hopegill Head. This is followed by elevated walking over Coledale Hause and on to the summit plateau of Grasmoor with its stunning views. Return is made over Wandope and by the narrow ridge of Whiteless Edge, over Whiteless Pike, with a steep descent towards Buttermere. Here you have the option to take in the easy, minor summit of Rannerdale Knotts with a return along the lane.*

Distance: *15.75km/9¾ miles.*

Height gained: *1,250m/4,100ft.*

Summits: *Whiteside, Hopegill Head, Grasmoor, Wandhope, Whiteless Pike, Rannerdale Knotts.*

Starting point: *Parking area at Lanthwaite Green near Crummock Water. Grid ref: NY 159 208.*

GRASMOOR HEADS A CLUTCH of bulky, rounded fells seen most frequently from the broad Derwent valley where it appears as a distant and fairly unimpressive high dome. To be 'wowed' by Grasmoor you need to see it from the south where it rises steeply above the picturesque Crummock Water as a 700-metre high pyramid of rock, scree and grass.

Ironically, most ascents are made from the east, but an ascent from Crummock Water taking in the narrow edges of Whiteside and Whiteless Pike is one of the classic rounds of the northern fells and a walk not to be missed.

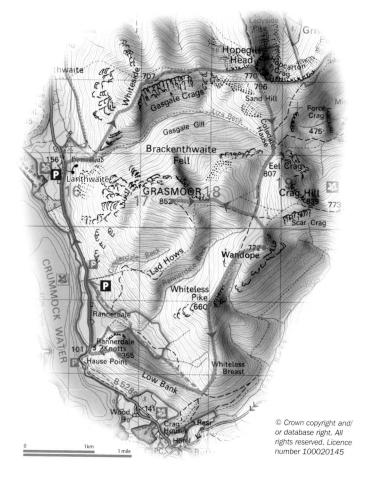

The route: Walk across the green—a broad rug of sheep-nibbled grass spreading out from the foot of the huge west face of Grasmoor—towards Gasgale Gill. The gill issues from the steep 'V'-shaped valley which separates Grasmoor and the craggy southern slopes of Whiteside. Cross the stream by a footbridge and take the path ahead to begin the steep, tiring ascent of Whiteside. The path is direct and steep but levels briefly on the minor summit of Whin Ben with its excellent views down to Crummock Water and across the patchwork of green fields to Loweswater. The path continues up the ridge, steepening again and giving widening views north across the Solway Firth to the Scottish Lowlands as you gain height.

The view east from Grasmoor to Whiteless Pike with the central fells on the skyline

Looking down to Crummock Water and Rannerdale Knotts from Grasmoor

The ascent ends abruptly on the summit of Whiteside, perched on the very brink Gasgale Crags, a wall of shattered rocks and gullies which fall almost from the ridge crest to Gasgale Gill 300m below.

With most of the ascent complete you can now cruise along the ridge towards the inviting summit of Hopegill Head. The ridge is a delight, easy-angled and narrow enough to be interesting without the need for any hands-on scrambling.

Hopegill Head feels like a true mountain summit, its pointed top perched on the brink of Hobcarton Crag. From here the ridge continues invitingly to Grisedale Pike, but our way heads right where a fork in the path leads away from the craggy crest and over the domed summit of Sand Hill to Coledale Hause where numerous paths converge. Take the main path ahead which climbs between the rounded slopes of Grasmoor on the right and Eel Crag on the left to the broad col at Wandope Moss.

At the broad crossing path turn right and rise, steeply at first, then more gently to Grasmoor's great domed summit, the highest point marked by a cairn.

This is a stunning viewpoint, the full 360 degree panorama dominated by the High Stile group beyond Buttermere, with Great Gable and Scafell Pike on the skyline.

Return to Wandope Moss. At the path junction, don't take the path right, go ahead for 50-100m or so, then bear right to the edge of the ridge and follow this to the summit of Wandope, little more than a stone's throw. From Wandope follow the good path along Whiteless Edge to Whiteless Pike, a fine pointed summit in a superb location overlooking Crummock Water. The view on all sides is to the sweeping grass edges so characteristic of this group of fells.

Continue the descent south down the broad grass ridge over Whiteless Breast to the level ground at the head of Rannerdale where the path splits. The path ahead leads down to Buttermere village; a right turn takes you down Rannerdale, or, for the most scenic finish bear right along the ridge (Low Bank) to the little summit of Rannerdale Knott, with its superb views of Crummock Water and Buttermere. *(For the Rannerdale option follow the path down the valley beside the beck then with fields on the left to the road.)*

For the Rannerdale Knott option, follow the path along the ridge crest to the summit directly above the lake. The path down to the road heads left from the summit. Turn right along the road back to Lanthwaite Green to complete the route.

The West

Scafell Pike and Scafell from the Mosedale Horseshoe

High Crag and High Stile from the head of Buttermere

6. *High Stile from Buttermere*

Outline: *Pleasant lakeside walking from Buttermere village to the head of the lake is followed by a moderate ascent to Scarth Gap. A steep climb on good paths then takes you onto the High Crag–High Stile ridge. Walking along the ridge is straightforward and easy-angled and there are grand views to Buttermere, Crummock Water and into Ennerdale. Descent from the ridge is by a steep, pitched path which needs care in wet conditions.*

Distance: *12.25km/7¾ miles.*

Height gained: *1,050m/3,430ft.*

Summits: *High Crag, High Stile, Red Pike.*

Starting point: *The village of Buttermere where there are two official car parks. Grid ref: NY 175 169.*

THERE ARE FEW LAKES so totally dominated by the adjacent fells than Buttermere by the High Stile group. In just over 1km/¾ mile, High Stile's steep northeastern slopes tumble over 600 metres to the wooded shores of the lake giving it the feel of a Norwegian Fjord.

The central location of these fells allows magnificent views over nearly all the Lakeland fells, particularly the nearby giants of the Scafell group; and just as the lake is dominated by the fells, a walk along the ridge is characterised by the ever-present bird's eye view' to Buttermere and Crummock Water.

The route: From the little bridge in the centre of Buttermere village, take the road beside the 'Bridge Hotel' and keep to the left of the 'Fish Hotel' along a gravel farm road towards the lake. Just before the lake, turn right to cross the footbridge over Buttermere Dubs—the river flowing out of Buttermere—and a second footbridge over Sourmilk Gill, which tumbles down the steep hillside above. Go through the hand gate and head left on the good path which keeps close to the lake

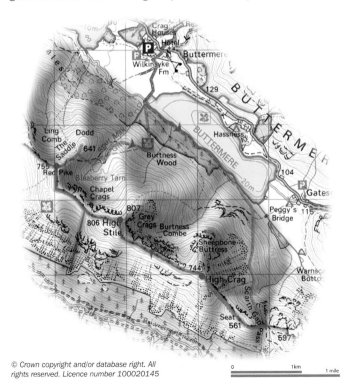

shore and through the conifer woods which cover the lower slopes of High Crag and High Stile.

There are good views from occasional breaks in the trees across to the house of Hassness in its wooded gardens and up to Fleetwith Pike dominating the valley head.

After the path leaves the woods and just before you reach the head of the lake, the path splits. Most traffic will keep ahead here on the popular lakeside trail, but our way heads right on the path which climbs diagonally up towards Haystacks and Scarth Gap (about 1.5km/1 mile).

As you gain height there are increasingly dramatic views. The soft green fields around Gatesgarth Farm contrast starkly with the craggy headwall of Warnscale Bottom and the dramatic northwest ridge of Fleetwith Pike which rises unbroken for almost 500m.

Soon the notch of Scarth Gap is visible ahead along with the jumbled northern crags of Haystacks. Just before you reach Scarth Gap a path breaks away on the right immediately before a wall but it is steep and isn't really worth the extra effort.

At Scarth Gap the hoped for view into the wilds of Ennerdale is not realised, the little pass being hemmed in on both sides. Great Gable and the rather unimpressive Kirk Fell being the only summits of note visible. The main pitched path bears left onto Haystacks now, but our way heads right up onto the little summit of Seat which gives you your first view of Ennerdale and Pillar. This is a better place for a stop than

The view to Crummock Water from High Stile

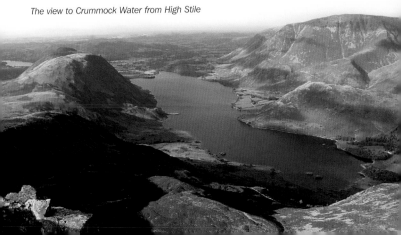

The summit of Dodd from the shoulder of Red Pike with Grasmoor behind

Scarth Gap, the views are wider and the crowds heading for Haystacks are now behind you.

The path dips a little after Seat, then climbs over 200m up Gamlin End to the summit of High Crag. This looks steep and it is—even with the stone pitching—prepare for some hard work.

The good news is that once the ascent to High Crag is behind you so is most of the hard work. The ridge ahead to High Stile is mainly level with just 50m ascent in a little over 1km/¾ mile, so stride out and enjoy the superb scenery on both sides of the ridge. To the right there are grand views into the shadowy depths of Burtness Combe and down to Buttermere lake over 600m below. The view left is out along the glacial trough of Ennerdale with the bulk of Pillar rising across the valley. Its famous rock, from which the whole mountain takes its name, is in the centre of the face directly below the summit.

As you reach the summit of High Stile walk ahead to the rim of the combe for one of the best views in the area. This takes in the full length of Crummock Water seen against the striking profiles of Red Pike and its smaller neighbour Dodd. It is also worth the short detour north for the view down the ridge to Buttermere village over 700m below.

The continuation to Red Pike is just as straightforward and follows the rim of the combe with fine views all the way. There is more grass on this section with just a short rise to the little stone wind shelter marking the highest point.

The initial descent northeast down the ridge from Red Pike is steep and very loose and requires care, but it is a short descent and soon you are on the easier ground of The Saddle—the broad rounded pass between Red Pike and the small summit of Dodd. This top is a short out-and-back detour and well worth it for the fine view down to Crummock Water and up to Fleetwith Pike at the head of the valley.

The path cuts diagonally down from The Saddle to cross the outflow stream from the tarn, then begins the steep descent to Birtness Woods by a tiring pitched path which requires care when wet. After crossing the stream the path swings leftwards coming close to the stone wall over on the left beside the stream. The pitching begins here and initially the angle is not great, but lower down it steepens considerably.

The reddish rock which gives the fell its name, is notoriously slippy when wet and on the steep sections the rocks have been placed parallel with the slope rather than forming steps. This path will not end soon enough, but by the time you enter Birtness Woods by the small gate the worst is behind you. The path cuts directly down through the trees and eventually joins the lakeside path beside the footbridge crossed earlier. Retrace the outward route back to Buttermere village to complete the route.

Fleetwith Pike seen at the head of Buttermere from Dodd

Fleetwith Pike from the Scarth Gap path

7. *Haystacks & Fleetwith Pike from Buttermere*

Outline: *A steady climb from the head of Buttermere leads to Scarth Gap—the high pass separating Buttermere from Ennerdale. A short section of steeper, rough walking leads to the summit of Haystacks with its sprinkling of tarns, rocky knolls and wide views. This is followed by easy walking between Haystacks and Fleetwith Pike (careful route finding needed on Fleetwith Pike) with a dramatic descent of Fleetwith Pike's northwest ridge.*

Distance: *7.25km/4½ miles.*

Height gained: *760m/2,500ft.*

Summits: *Haystacks, Fleetwith Pike.*

Starting point: *The little car park at Gatesgarth Farm at the foot of the Honister Pass. Grid ref: NY 196 150.*

THE SUPERB LITTLE FELL which hides itself at the head of Buttermere between the soaring profile of Fleetwith Pike and the High Stile range owes its current popularity to the late Alfred Wainwright, the famous guidebook writer and illustrator. In life it was his favourite fell in the whole of the Lake District and it has become his final resting place. On his request his ashes were scattered here following his death in 1991 at the age of 84.

This route combines the pleasant traverse of Haystacks with the drama of Fleetwith Pike and a descent of its impressive northwest ridge.

The route: From Gatesgarth Farm, take the signed bridleway beside the little bridge opposite the car park. This passes the beside the farm before heading out across the flat valley floor with the dramatic prow of High Crag rising ahead. Cross the footbridge over the Warnscale Beck and after the kissing gate take the rising footpath ahead beside the woods (the path right is the lakeside trail). At the end of the woods turn left on the path up to Scarth Gap.

As you gain height there are increasingly dramatic views to both Haystacks and Fleetwith Pike, the latter rising dramatically above the flats of Warnscale Bottom.

Scarth Gap is a junction of trails. The path ahead leads down into the head of Ennerdale, the path right swings up onto the High Stile ridge and the path left (likely carrying the most traffic) leads up onto Haystacks. The path is pitched all the way even on the rocky sections which will require a steadying hand here and there.

Innominate Tarn and Great Gable

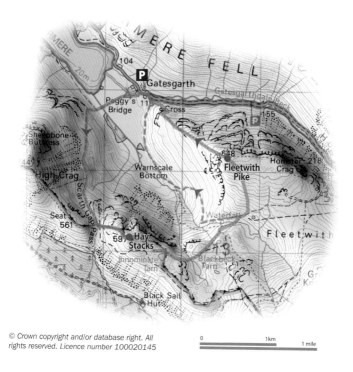

0   1km

1 mile

The summit of Haystacks is surprisingly intricate, a jumble of rocky knolls separated by boggy hollows or small tarns. These provide excellent foregrounds for wide views in all directions, the most dramatic being along the full length of Ennerdale with Pillar, Kirk Fell and Great Gable dominating the valley head.

There are several paths around the summit so things can be a little confusing, however, in all but the poorest visibility Innominate Tarn, the next objective, can be seen about 500m to the southeast. The main footpath heads for this passing along the northern (left-hand) shore.

In warm sunny weather this is certainly a place to linger and it is easy to understand why Wainwright enjoyed being here so much. It was along the shore of this tarn that his ashes were scattered.

The path continues southeast and after a short descent, where you will enjoy a superb view down the Buttermere valley, crosses Black Beck, the stream flowing from Blackbeck Tarn up to the right. At a fork just above the beck keep right and follow the good path gently descending for about 500m or so. A path breaks left here heading down into Warnscale Bottom but the main path swings right towards quarry spoil. Stay with the main path soon crossing Warnscale Beck in the broad marshy hollow of Dubs Bottom. Take the path ahead here which rises up towards the quarry spoil seen earlier. Look for 'Dubs Bothy', a stone refuge and bothy beyond a rough quarry road.

(If you want to cut the route short leaving Fleetwith Pike for another day, take the path on the left immediately before Dubs Bothy. This heads down beside Warnscale Beck to Warnscale Bottom returning to Gatesgarth.)

To continue, pass to the right of Dubs Bothy and walk ahead up a small grass rake between areas of mining spoil. Continue up past

The stunning view from Fleetwith Pike to Buttermere and Crummock Water

Haystacks from the head of Buttermere

a small square wind shelter (quarry over to the right) on a faint path towards a larger heap of spoil. Pass this on the right following a faint path which soon swings leftwards. The path becomes better established as you continue on a diagonal line over the undulating ground to the summit of Fleetwith Pike.

As you would imagine Fleetwith Pike is a superb viewpoint with an unrivalled view down the valley to Buttermere and Crummock Water, the High Stile ridge to the south and the Derwent Fells to the north. Immediately to the north is the Honister Pass, a dizzying 400m below.

The descent is by the northwest ridge, known as Fleetwith Edge, which provides such a striking sight from almost anywhere in the Buttermere valley. You can't see down the ridge from the summit so descend a little for the best view. Although the edge is a straightforward path, the upper section does require a little scrambling here and there. Once you are off the rocks the rest of the ridge is a straightforward grass path.

Almost at the bottom of the ridge the path swings right to avoid the rocks of Low Raven Crag. At the road turn left back to the car park to complete the route.

Scafell Pike and Scafell from Red Pike

8. Scafell Pike & Great End from Wasdale Head

Outline: *From Wasdale Head a well-used path rises to Sty Head pass where many routes converge. Easy walking on good paths continues to Esk Hause and finally the high ridge crest just south of Great End, the first summit of the day. The walk along the broad ridge takes in Ill Crag, Broad Crag and finally Scafell Pike, the highest point in England. The final summit of the day is an easy jaunt over the broad connecting ridge with a steep descent back to Wasdale Head.*

Distance: *14.25km/8¾ miles.*

Height gained: *1,170m/3,830ft.*

Summits: *Great End, Scafell Pike, Lingmell.*

Starting point: *There is a large parking area at Wasdale Green, about 400m before the famous 'Wasdale Head Inn'.*
Grid ref: NY 186 084.

WASDALE IS ONE OF MOST impressive valleys in the Lake District, with England's highest summit and deepest lake almost side by side. It also has one of the most famous mountain views in Britain—the summits of Yewbarrow, Great Gable and the Scafell group rising beyond Wast Water. With these top attractions you would think the place would be packed, but Wasdale is also one of the most remote valley heads in the Lake District—the long drive from the main tourist centres of Ambleside and Keswick keeping the crowds to a minimum.

Starting at Wasdale Head, this route explores the highest group of summits in England culminating in Scafell Pike—a fine handful of Lakeland giants.

The route: From the northern end of the green take the walled farm lane beside 'Lingmell House'. This leads between the small walled-fields which are so characteristic of Wasdale Head, past the tiny church of Saint Olaf to Burnthwaite Farm. Bear left as signed immediately before the farm and pass between the outbuildings to continue on a good

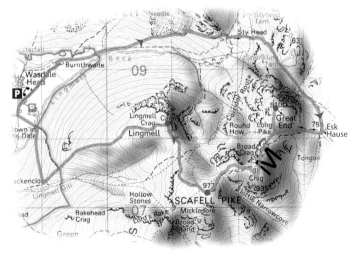

0   1km   1 mile

Looking up to Scafell Pike and Lingmell from Sty Head

path with the commanding prospect of Great Gable rising ahead. The bridleway crosses a footbridge over Gable Beck, then runs tight below the long southern slopes of the mountain beside the tumbling Lingmell Beck. At a fork, keep left on the higher path. *(Both paths lead to Sty Head but the left-hand option makes a more even climb and gives grand views back to Wasdale Head.)*

As you climb higher the impressive prow of Lingmell, the final summit of the day, rears up across the valley and there are impressive views looking back to the handfull of buildings at Wasdale Head dwarfed by the surrounding fells.

Sty Head pass is the meeting of many routes. Old pack horse trails linking Wasdale with Borrowdale and Langdale, used this high pass and you will often see tents beside Sty Head Tarn. The high point of the pass is marked by a large boulder and mountain rescue box. Take the path on the right here which climbs gently to Sprinkling Tarn, another popular camping spot cradled in a grassy hollow below the dark brooding north face of Great End which rises over 300m above the lake.

The path ahead continues the moderate climb to Esk Hause, 1km/¾ mile distant and famous for lying at the very centre of the Lakeland fells. In the approach to the hause bear right at a fork *(the left fork leads to a slightly lower pass separating Esk Hause from the summit of Allen Crags—worth the short detour if you are collecting summits.*

Esk Hause lies at the head of upper Esk Dale one of the wildest and most remote valleys in the Lake District and surrounded by Lakeland's highest fells. In clear conditions its impressive setting can be appreciated fully—Esk Pike and Bowfell on the left and the impressive Ill Crag—one of Scafell Pike's satellites—on the right.

Turn right here on the path which leads up through the little hollow of Calf Cove and onto the broad ridge. Turn right for Great End, 300-400m north across the plateau. Predictably, it is a superb viewpoint, particularly for Great Gable and Wasdale Head, but also for the castellated crags of Lingmell. You can also see the entire route from here—the broad rocky ridge linking Great End with Scafell Pike, along with the outliers of Ill Crag and Broad Crag.

Retrace your steps, then follow the broad path southwest. Straightforward enough in clear conditions, less so in the mist, although there are frequent cairns and the path is well worn.

The path to Esk Hause with the shapely summit of Ill Crag rising behind

The view to Lingmell backed by Pillar, Red Pike and Kirk Fell from Great End

The main path bypasses the summits of Ill Crag and Broad Crag, both requiring short detours. Make sure you don't miss the pointed summit of Ill Crag—this top is worth the detour mainly for the stunning view down the mountain's southern face into the wilds of upper Esk Dale, the snaking river seen against the impressive rock summit of Pen. It also provides a better resting place than Scafell Pike as the latter attracts the crowds and can be a busy spot even on the quietest of days.

Beyond Broad Crag a drop to the little pass at the head of Little Narrowcove followed by a short scrambly ridge and you are on the highest summit in England.

As already mentioned the summit is rarely crowd free and its large cain will likely be littered with visitors. A far better resting place is the summit of Ill Crag.

From Scafell Pike take the good cairned footpath which heads northwest. Ignore the path which soon breaks away left. This leads to Mickledore and Scafell. The path descends to Lingmell Col before the rise to the final summit of the day. *The broad Hollow Stones path breaks away left here which can used if time is pressing,* otherwise continue ahead up the ridge to Lingmell, an easy 100m rise.

Lingmell probably has the best situation of all the summits on the Scafell range. The northern cliffs fall almost 300m and the steep slopes below another 300m to Lingmell Beck, but across the valley the imposing bulk of Great Gable steals the show, quite an achievement in such an impressive setting.

Descend by the path which heads west for about 1km/¾ mile to join the steep, rounded grassy ridge which drops beside Lingmell Gill. Don't descend all the way to the gill, instead take the path which strikes rightwards about halfway down the ridge to make a diagonal descent of the hillside to the footbridge over Lingmell Beck. Cross the bridge and follow the path ahead back to Wasdale Green to complete the route.

Descending from Scafell Pike to Lingmell backed by Great End

Scafell from Cam Spout

9. *Scafell from Eskdale*

Outline: *A long, beautiful approach to the mountain through upper Eskdale and beside the infant River Esk. This is followed by steep walking and occasional scrambling to reach a remote mountain hollow. A choice of routes takes you steeply to the summit. Return is made by a descent of the mountain's southern slopes followed by a long walk over moors and upland pastures.*

Distance: *14km/8³/₄ miles.*

Height gained: *1,200m/3,900ft.*

Summits: *Scafell, Slight Side.*

Starting point: *Laybys or a small car park at the foot of the Hardknott Pass in Eskdale. Grid ref: NY 212 011.*

SCAFELL PIKE MAY HAVE THE CROWN as England's highest summit, but Scafell has the more mountain-like form. It is possibly the most inaccessible of the Lake District's major summits, ringed on three sides by impressive cliff scenery.

Though one of the toughest, this route is undoubtedly the best approach to the mountain offering the chance to sample the delights of the wildly beautiful upper Eskdale valley.

The route: The Eskdale path leaves the lane at the foot of the Hard-knott Pass where there is an old phone box beside the access road to 'Brotherilkeld Farm' (NT). Keep to the left of the farm taking the path beside the River Esk. Ignore a footbridge which crosses the river on the left keeping ahead below scattered oaks which frame views ahead to a very shapely Bowfell.

Soon fields give way to open moors but the path continues beside the river, a beautiful ribbon of cascades and deep pools which would be hard to resist on a hot day.

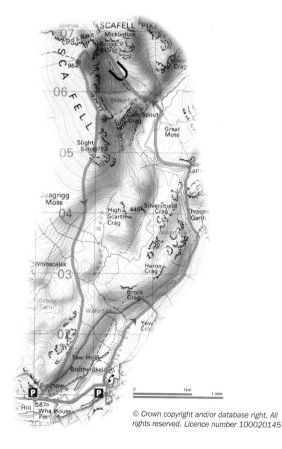

Scafell Pike and Ill Crag from the River Esk

The valley narrows a little as you approach Lingcove Bridge—a picturesque stone arch spanning Lingcove Beck—below the little rocky summit of Throstlehow Crag. Once across the bridge the hard work begins with a steep climb beside the Esk Falls. The path emerges in a marshy hollow on a bend of the river with a view ahead and left to Scafell and Scafell Pike for the first time. The path swings left with the river then, where the river bends left, take a left off the main path crossing a stream to stay with the Esk as it snakes into the wild upper reaches of the valley and below the crags of Scar Lathing.

Soon the valley opens out into a wide plain—a great hidden valley which comes as quite a surprise. You should now be able to see the route ahead clearly—the crag-lined ridge to the left is the Cam Spout Ridge and at its foot the waterfall of Cam Spout issuing from the hidden combe above. The flat expanse below this is known as the Great Moss, a mix of streams, pools and peat bog which can be difficult to cross during a sustained wet period. The two pointed summits ahead are Scafell Pike and Ill Crag. Scafell is now out of view.

Stay more or less beside the river heading towards Cam Spout. This can be very wet at times so you will have to be creative with the line you take. Watch for a suitable place to cross the river (usually easier when you are directly opposite Cam Spout) and once on the far side head directly towards Cam Spout.

The path ascends the slabby rocks to the right of the falls with the best but hardest scrambling directly adjacent to the gorge. The scrambling is easier with little or no exposure further right.

The path emerges in the upper combe and in good visibility you should be able to see the final section of the route ahead. The usual route from here takes the obvious well-worn path ahead on a direct line up towards the saddle on the skyline known as Mickledore. Unfortunately there is no walker's route from there to Scafell so, before you reach Mickledore, and immediately before Scafell's eastern cliffs which rise impressively on the left, look for an easy looking square-cut gully on the left with a cairn at the bottom. Scramble up this gully beside the stream. The scrambling is easy, there are no drops and the stream leads to the tiny pool (no where near large enough to have its own name) known as Foxes Tarn.

Above the tarn a path zig-zags up scree to the summit plateau. Here and there remains of an older pitched path can be seen but most of this has disappeared into the moving scree.

On the upper section of the Cam Spout Ridge with the wilds of upper Eskdale below

The summit plateau is surprisingly broad and spacious like its more famous neighbour, although here you will have a much better chance of being alone. The rock scenery around the sub-top of Symond's Knott and Scafell Crag to the north is stunning.

The main summit is 100m to the south. The view is similar to that from Scafell Pike but is more dominated by the sea. The deep glacial hollow of Mosedale beyond Wasdale Head is particularly impressive.

An alternative to this final section if you want to avoid the crowds is the Cam Spout Ridge. For this option bear left to cross the stream as soon as you finish the scrambling beside Cam Spout. Make your way up steep, grassy, pathless ground with occasional rocky steps to reach the rounded ridge crest. Follow this to the summit ridge and turn right along the broken ridge to reach Scafell.

From Scafell head southeast along the ridge with grand views down into the void of upper Eskdale 500m below. Pass over the sup-top of Long Green and continue down to the final summit of the day, Slight Side. There are excellent views back to the Scafell group from here.

Descend the steep rocky southern slopes of Slight Side overlooking the vast expanse of Quagrigg Moss. The steep ground and scree soon give way to easier-angled grass and a good path heads almost due south (towards Harter Fell). At a fork the Boot path breaks right. Ignore this, continuing ahead eventually crossing Catcove Beck. Keep to the most obvious path ahead now for a gentle finish ideal for tired legs. The path finally passes through stone sheep pens to reach a small car park adjacent to the lane. Turn left for a 1km/¾ mile return along the lane to complete the route.

Long Green, Slight Side and Ill Crag from the end of the walk

Mosedale with Pillar, Red Pike and Yewbarrow from Scafell

10. *The Mosedale Horseshoe from Wasdale Head*

Outline: *A gradual climb on a good path from Wasdale Head to Black Sail Pass is followed by a high-level ridge walk to Pillar and Scoat Fell. (For better views and a close-up view of the famous Pillar rock there is a traversing path on the north side of Pillar.) The broad ridge continues to Red Pike and finally a scramble both onto and off the superb little mountain of Yewbarrow to complete the round.*

Distance: *17.25km/11 miles.*

Height gained: *1,630m/5,350ft.*

Summits: *Pillar, Scoat Fell, Steeple, Red Pike, Yewbarrow.*

Starting point: *There is a large parking area at Wasdale Green, about 400m before the famous 'Wasdale Head Inn'. Grid ref: NY 186 084.*

WASDALE HEAD IS ONE OF the most famous centres for both walking and climbing in the region and is noted for being the brithplace of rock climbing which began here way back in the 1880s with an ascent of

Napes Needle on Great Gable. Its reputation is well earned, the wildest valley head in the Lake District, surrounded by it's highest summits. But nearly all eyes are turned by either Scafell Pike—the highest summit in England—or by the equally famous Great Gable, leaving one of the finest horseshoe walks in the region unnoticed and almost untouched little more than a stone's throw away.

This is a superb route over high ground, gathering a fine collection of Lakeland summits along the way and enjoying unrivalled views of the Scafell group throughout.

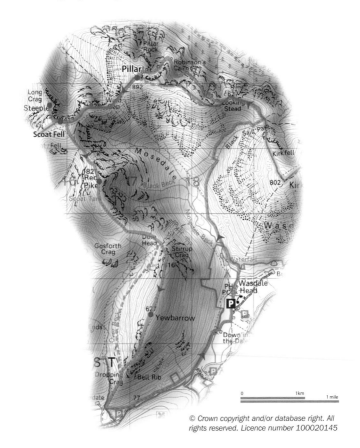

Pillar rising at the head of the wild, empty valley of Mosedale at the start of the walk

The route: From Wasdale Green follow the lane to the 'Wasdale Head Inn'. Turn left through the car park past the shop and bar and bear right beside the beck. Pass the picturesque little stone bridge continuing ahead between the beck and a farm on the right. Soon the path splits—bear left rising to a gate where the Mosedale path swings left again (the steep path directly ahead leads to the summit of Kirk Fell).

Soon you are in the wilds of Mosedale and you can appreciate just how large and impressive it is for the first time. At the head of the dale the south face of Pillar rises in a series of steep broken crags over 700m, with the craggy eastern face of Red Pike to the left. Looking back there is a fine view to Wasdale Head with the pointed summit of Symond's Knott on Scafell peeping over the shoulder of Lingmell.

The path soon curves rightwards to begin the long climb to Black Sail Pass. Once you have crossed Gatherstone Beck the view back down the valley becomes increasingly impressive as the northern prow of Yewbarrow soars 500m above the beck, culminating in Stirrup Crags which will provide the final scramble of the day.

As you reach the summit of the pass, the extensive view hoped for is not realised, so head left along the ridge making the minor detour right to the summit of Looking Stead and all will be revealed—the shadowy forested depths of Ennerdale, the Haystacks/High Stile ridge, with Fleetwith Pike and the Robinson/Hinscarth ridge beyond. Southwards, it is the striking prow of Yewbarrow which once again grabs the eye.

Beyond the little grassy col immediately after Looking Stead the ridge steepens and you have a choice. A few metres above the col there is a cairn marking the start of the 'Climber's Traverse' or 'High Level Route'. This is a path which breaks right and traverses across the steep northern flanks of Pillar to the famous Robinson's Cairn with its stunning views of Pillar Rock. From Robinson's Cairn the path swings leftwards zig-zaging up a short scree slope to gain the end of an easy-angled rake which is followed, with a little exposure onto Shamrock, almost level with the summit of Pillar Rock. From here the path takes a steep line leftwards up the broken slopes to the summit. There is no difficulty on this route and only here and there is there any real exposure, but it will not be for everyone. It is a must if you want to see Pillar Rock close up.

The alternative to the 'Climber's Traverse' is to continue steeply up the ridge from Looking Stead to the summit of Pillar. You will still enjoy spectacular views into both Ennerdale and Mosedale from the ridge but you will miss out on the intimate views of Pillar Rock.

Pillar has one of the best panoramas in the Lake District, a prospect dominated mainly by the jumbled, rocky mass of the Scafell group to

On the summit of Looking Stead with Yewbarrow in the distance

Setting off towards Pillar Rock from Robinson's Cairn

the southeast, with the distinctive profile of Great Gable seen over the rounded back of Kirk Fell. Westwards, the view takes in the long glacial trough of Ennerdale culminating in Ennerdale Water with the Irish Sea in the distance.

From Pillar, head southwest over the extensive summit plateau and descend into Wind Gap, the pass separating Pillar from Black Crag. *(The unappealing scree chute to the left provides a safe escape route back into Mosedale should you need to cut the route short.)* The climb to Black Crag is broken and rocky but soon over and the remaining ridge to Scoat Fell is narrow and grassy with just a short rise over rocks to the summit, an unremarkable stony plateau crossed by a stone wall *(Scoat Fell can be avoided by a contouring path from the grassy col).*

If you opted for the climb to Scoat Fell, the out and back extension to the superb summit of Steeple is recommended. Steeple will have caught your eye back on the summit of Pillar and by the time you reach Scoat Fell will have become a must do. The sight of Steeple as you approach along the ridge backed by Ennerdale and High Stile is one of the highlights of the walk. The summit is quite a contrast to

Two walkers on the summit of Steeple

the expansive caps of the neighbouring fells and perched on the brink of the massive fall into Mirk Cove, Steeple feels more like an Alpine summit than a Lakeland fell.

Return to Scoat Fell and head southeast to pick up the ridge path to Red Pike. Although the summit is mainly grass, the cascade of crags falling 600m into Mosedale to the northeast give it more of a mountain feel than its neighbours. Again the view is dominated by the Scafell group across the divide of Wasdale, but looking down the ridge ahead you can now see the final summit of the day and from here it does not look straightforward. You can now see that the rocks of Stirrup Crag wrap around the northern spur of the mountain and will require scrambling if you are to stay on the ridge.

The descent to the pass of Dore Head is by a mix of grass and scree, a good, visible path all the way. Here you have a choice again. To maintain the character of the route Yewbarrow must be included and makes a superb finale, but, like the Climber's Traverse on Pillar, may not be to everyone's liking requiring simple scrambling in both ascent and descent.

Alternatives from here are either to descend the steep screes to the left—straightforward but requiring care, or to head right more easily on the path beside Over Beck. This passes below Dropping Crag to reach the car park at Overbeck Bridge.

For the Yewbarrow option, ascend directly up the broken, loose slope to begin the short scramble onto the ridge. The easiest line is on the left edge of the crags almost overlooking the drop into Mosedale. There is less exposure to the right but the scrambling is less straightforward.

The summit ridge is a grand grass platform from which to view the day's achievements and enjoy yet more views of the Scafell group. The highest point is towards the southern end of the ridge, the last summit of the day.

The descent is initially straightforward and heads down the narrowing ridge with superb views to Wast Water over 500m below backed by the impressive wall of screes which fall into the lake from Illgill Head. Lower down look for the point where the path breaks right above Dropping Crag. This is important as there is no walking route down the ridge crest from here. The descent is now steep and loose and you may doubt you are in the right place, but the path is obvious and there is a short section of formalised pitching lower down. At the bottom of the scree a path heads left through the bracken to cross a ladder stile on the grassy ridge crest. Looking back up the ridge you will see the reason for the diversion. Head right down the grass path beside the wall to a second stile. (*This is where the Over Beck route joins*.) Turn left here and follow the path down beside the beck to the little car park.

The return to Wasdale Head is unavoidably along the road—just over 2km/1½ miles.

Superb views to the Scafell group with Yewbarrow nearer at hand

Great Gable from Lingmell

11. Great Gable & Kirk Fell from Wasdale Head

Outline: *From Wasdale Head a good path rises to Sty Head pass where many routes converge. A traversing path is then taken across the high face of Great Gable with stunning views and some easy scrambling. Steep, stony paths lead over Great Gable and its smaller neighbour Green Gable with easier walking north over grassy moors towards Brandreth. The scenic path known as Moses Trod then leads back to Beck Head pass followed by an ascent of Kirk Fell. The broad ridge is followed to Black Sail Pass with a return to Wasdale Head through the wild valley head of Mosedale.*

Distance: *18.75km/9¾ miles.*

Height gained: *1,325m/4,350ft.*

Summits: *Great Gable, Green Gable, Kirk Fell.*

Starting point: *There is a large parking area at Wasdale Green, about 400m before the famous 'Wasdale Head Inn'.*
Grid ref: NY 186 084.

Wᴀsᴅᴀʟᴇ ɪs ᴊᴜsᴛɪғɪᴀʙʟʏ ʀᴇɢᴀʀᴅᴇᴅ as Lakeland's most impressive valley—and how could it not be, with England's deepest lake and highest summit almost side by side, along with one of Britain's classic mountain views—the summits of Yewbarrow, Great Gable and the Scafell group rising beyond West Water.

Great Gable is the centrepiece in this view and this route searches out a devious line on the fell's impressive southern slopes, passing close to the crags where the sport of rock climbing began, with a more gentle finish on Kirk Fell. Options for simplifying or shortening the route are included.

The route: From the northern end of the green take the walled farm lane beside 'Lingmell House'. This leads between the small walled-fields which are so characteristic of Wasdale Head, past the tiny church of Saint Olaf to Burnthwaite Farm. Bear left as signed immediately before

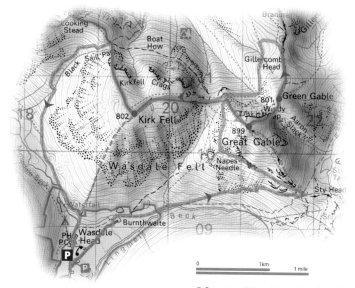

Great End from the Sty Head path

the farm and pass between the outbuildings to continue on a good path with the commanding prospect of Great Gable rising ahead. Cross the footbridge over Gable Beck (ignoring the path which heads left almost immediately) continuing ahead on the path which keeps tight below the long southern slopes of the mountain beside the tumbling Lingmell Beck. At a fork keep left on the higher path. *(Both paths lead to Sty Head but the left-hand option makes a more even climb and gives grand views back to Wasdale Head.)*

Sty Head pass is crossed by numerous paths and makes a good resting place. Old pack horse trails linking Wasdale with Borrowdale and Langdale, used this high pass and you will often see tents beside Sty Head Tarn. The high point of the pass is marked by a large boulder and mountain rescue box. *(The easiest and most straightforward route to Great Gable from here is to take the pitched path left by the mountain rescue box. The route is straightforward but uninteresting and there are many false summit to dishearten you on the way.)*

A much more interesting route is by the path known as the 'Climber's Traverse' which contours across the mountain's steep southern face high above Wasdale Head with spectacular views into the valley. There is also some easy scrambling as you pass beneath the famous Napes Needle and Sphinx rocks. Both rocks have strong links with the early history of rock climbing (the remarkable solo ascent of Napes Needle in 1886 by W.P. Hasket-Smith is considered to be the first true rock climb).

For the 'Climber's Traverse' take the pitched path left by the mountain rescue box, but bear left after a few metres on a less distinct path which rises diagonally up for 100m or so before becoming better defined at a point where you can see down towards Wasdale Head again. The path contours easily towards the crag known as Kern Knotts with its distinctive vertical crack, first climbed in 1897 by the Welsh rock climber, Owen Glyn Jones. Scramble over the large boulders below the crag and continue across the wide screes which follow.

The next crags (Great Napes) are much higher and after a scree gully the path skirts the foot of the steep face passing over broken rocks with short sections of easy scrambling. The situation is superb—the screes fall away to Lingmell Beck 450m below and there is a superb view down to Wasdale Head where the walk started—and shortly the famous Napes Needle comes into view above.

There are superb views from Great Gable down to Wast Water and Wasdale Head

Kirk Fell, Pillar and Scoat Fell from the summit of Great Gable

Napes Needle is not immediately obvious from below as it tends to merge into the face above and the well known view is from the opposite direction. This can be reached by ascending the scree gully beyond to a point almost level with the base of the needle. *Alternatively, competent scramblers can climb over the gap at the back of the needle and make the short descent to the gully (known as 'threading the needle'), but don't attempt this unless you are confident scrambling in such situations and you are sure of your location.*

The contouring path continues below Napes Needle and across the broken rocks which follow, to cross a wide scree slope or gully separating the crags of Great Napes and the smaller White Napes. This brings you to crest of the rounded ridge which rises up from Wasdale Head. The path continues to contour to Beck Head, the pass between Great Gable and Kirk Fell. From here a steep, rocky, but clear path rises up the ridge to the right to the summit of Great Gable.

After the steep terrain of the 'Climber's Traverse' the summit comes as something of surprise being little more than the high point in a wide rocky plateau, although its central location gives it a fine panorama in all directions.

In clear conditions it is worth including the adjacent summit of Green Gable, otherwise you will need to retrace your route back to Beck Head to include Kirk Fell. For Green Gable take the cairned path northeast and soon you will be looking down to Windy Gap, the little col which separates the two summits. Descend into the gap and make the short rise to Green Gable.

From here you could drop back into the gap and take the path right down scree to join the path which skirts below the dark face of Gable Crag. In good visibility however, a better option is to take the path north to the broad saddle of Gillercomb Head, the low point on the broad ridge separating Green Gable from Brandreth, where there are a few small pools. From here swing left to join the contouring path known as 'Moses Trod'.

In good visibility you will enjoy superb views into the head of Ennerdale from here, its great 'U'-shaped form contrasting with the angular crags of Pillar Rock high on Pillar mountain. From a little higher on the ridge you will also have good views into the Buttermere valley separated by the High Stile ridge.

On the direct descent to Wasdale Head from Kirk Fell

Follow the 'Moses Trod' path into Stone Cove below Gable Crag and continue up to Beck Head again. Now for the final summit of the day *(you could of course descend from here by taking the path ahead back to Wasdale Head)*. The rise to Kirk Fell follows the rounded, stony slopes to the right, the climb from the pass being just under 200m. The summit is a spacious grassy moor with the highest point not immediately obvious. There are in fact two summits separated by a handful of small tarns. The highest is to the west and both are crossed by the line of old fence posts which provide a useful guide in misty conditions.

Kirk Fell offers stunning views down into Wasdale Head—with its a 'bird's eye view' of the hotel and adjacent farms—and along the valley to Wast Water. You are also much closer to Pillar and the ring of summits forming the classic round known as the Mosedale Horseshoe—Pillar, Scoat Fell, Red Pike and Yewbarrow (route 10).

There are two main options for a descent back to Wasdale. You could continue along the ridge heading north with the old fence posts to Black Sail Pass, then turn south (left) into Mosedale and follow the good well-marked footpath through Mosedale to Wasdale Head. *Alternatively, if you are impatient to get down as soon as possible, a shorter but much steeper descent can be made by heading southwest from the summit on a path which soon steepens dramatically covering the full 700m to the valley in little more than 1.5km/1 mile.*

The East

Harter Fell and Hawswater

Helvellyn from Striding Edge

12. Helvellyn by Striding Edge & Swirral Edge

Outline: **SCRAMBLE** *Easy walking to Lanty's Tarn to gain the Grisedale path followed by a long moderate ascent to the ridge crest. Straightforward low-grade scrambling on a narrow rock ridge with some exposure to reach Helvellyn's high summit plateau. A shorter scrambling descent via Swirral Edge, then easier walking to the shapely summit of Catstycam. The long easy-angled Glenridding path provides a return route.*

Distance: *12km/7½ miles.*

Height gained: *960m/3,150ft.*

Summits: *Helvellyn, Catstycam.*

Starting point: *The National Park car park in the centre of Glenridding. Grid ref: NY 385 169.*

THE MOST FAMOUS AND POPULAR mountains and hills in any area are usually the highest—Snowdon in North Wales, Ben Nevis in Scotland—but in the Lake District Helvellyn seems to have jumped the queue and knocked Scafell Pike off the number one spot. One reason for this is undoubtedly the inaccessibility of the latter—tucked away in the far west, well away from the main tourist routes. Helvellyn, on the other hand, rises directly from a main road which runs through the heart of the district. It is also one of the four highest summits in the Lake District and it has perhaps the most famous ridge walk in the country—Striding Edge. This narrow airy arête is justifiably famous and provides one of the best mountain experiences to be had on the Lakeland fells.

The route: Leave the car park by the lower entrance and turn right along the road to cross the bridge. Turn right immediately (opposite the 'Glenridding Hotel') and walk along the lane between the river and the shops. At the end of the access lane go through the large gate ahead and in a few metres cross the footbridge on the left. Follow the pitched footpath up through woods and onto the open hillside.

At a gate in the wall ahead, don't go through, instead turn sharp left and follow the path up to Lanty's Tarn, in its small hollow and surrounded by pines. There are good views back down to Ullswater just before you enter the woods.

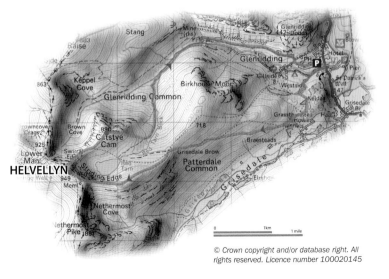

Looking to Helvellyn from the approach to Striding Edge in remarkable winter conditions

Follow the path past the tarn, then bear right off the main path on a narrower footpath which heads across grass to enter and pass through a small wood by gates. Beyond the wood the path descends to join the main path coming up from Grisedale.

There are superb views from here up to the head of the valley to the shapely summits of Nethermost Pike, Dolywaggon Pike and St Sunday Crag.

Turn right and follow the broad path which climbs steadily up towards the famous 'Hole in the Wall'—a gap in the wall which can be seen running up the hillside to the skyline ahead. The path is never steep but it is much further than it looks to the skyline (over 2km/1½ miles).

As you gain height there are increasing views left into Grisedale and up to the head of the valley.

The ridge crest is a good place for a break. Here the impressive east face of Helvellyn, with the enclosing arms of Striding Edge and Swirral Edge, can be seen for the first time rising above Red Tarn which occupies the bottom of the combe (out of sight until you are further along the ridge).

Cross the stile here ('Hole in the Wall') and continue on the path ahead. Striding Edge starts with the small summit of Low Spying How, a good place to take stock of the ridge ahead. The first section is composed of clean blocky rock with very little grass, the second half is narrower with a sharper crest but more broken rocks. No where is the scrambling difficult but it is fairly exposed, so you will need good balance and a head for heights. The less adventurous can avoid the crest by a traversing path a little way down on the right.

The final obstacle on the ridge provides the crux—a squat rock tower requiring a short scramble descent to a narrow gap at the point where the ridge merges into the broken upper slopes of the mountain. Easier scrambling, then steep scree lead onto the summit plateau where you will enjoy the fine classic view back along the ridge.

Head right along the plateau rim past the cross-shaped stone wind shelter to the summit marked by a triangulation pillar.

Helvellyn is one of the few Lakeland summits where almost every other fell is visible. The most striking panorama is westwards, where you should be able to see the Coniston Fells, Bowfell, Crinkle Crags, Esk Pike and Scafell Pike. Great Gable is probably the most prominent and striking of all. The Derwent Fells and Skiddaw complete the view to the northwest.

Looking back along Striding Edge from the final ascent to the summit

Beginning the descent of Swirral Edge with Catstycam in the background

Looking back to Helvellyn and Swirral Edge from Catstycam

Beyond the summit a small cairn marks the exit point from the plateau onto Swirral Edge. This is both easier and shorter than Striding Edge, the broken rocks soon merging into grass as the angle eases on the broad saddle between Helvellyn and Catstycam. A good path bears right from here to the outflow of the lake where it joins the Glenridding path, but Catstycam is too good a summit to leave out and is easily gained by the gentle ridge ahead.

The view back to Helvellyn rising above Red Tarn from here is superb, particularly under winter conditions, or when late snow lingers on this sheltered northeast face.

From the summit, descend the rounded east ridge on the path which sweeps down to join the Glenridding path beside Red Tarn Beck. Follow this path left down to the Youth Hostel where a wooden footbridge on the left crosses the main stream. Cross this, passing the outdoor centre and Youth Hostel to join the unsurfaced lane which can be followed easily back to Glenridding to complete the route (about 2km/1½ miles).

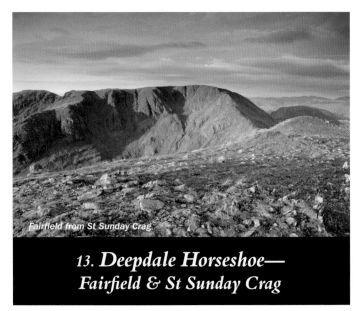

Fairfield from St Sunday Crag

13. *Deepdale Horseshoe—* *Fairfield & St Sunday Crag*

Outline: *After a gentle start in Patterdale, a steep climb up Thornhow End takes you onto the broad stocky summit ridge of St Sunday Crag with its superb views of Helvellyn and its impressive eastern ridges. With much of the height gained the walking is easier along the ridge with a short simple scramble over Cofa Pike to reach Fairfield's broad summit plateau. The broad ridge is followed to Hart Crag, then abandoned in favour of the long gentle arm of Hartsop Above How with its excellent views into the wilds of upper Deepdale.*

Distance: *14.5km/9miles.*

Height gained: *1050m/3,400ft.*

Summits: *St Sunday Crag, Fairfield, Hart Crag, Hartsop Above How (Birks optional).*

Starting point: *Small pay and display car park opposite the 'Patterdale Hotel', Patterdale. Grid ref: NY 396 159.*

FAIRFIELD SITS AT THE CENTRE of a complex of fells, ridges and dales running to all points of the compass. With several close neighbours, some major summits in themselves, the Fairfield group is perfect for ridge walking and boasts two of the best 'horseshoe' rounds in the region—the Fairfield Horseshoe (Route 16) which takes in the southern ridges centred on Rydal and the Deepdale Horseshoe to the northeast.

The route: From the car park cross the road and walk through the hotel car park keeping to the right of the main building. Take the signed footpath behind the hotel which passes through a small wood to a kissing gate. Go through the gate and bear right to follow a contouring path for about 1km/¾ mile.

At a path junction immediately below the steep, blunt ridge of Thornhow End (grid ref: NY 387 157), turn left. The path is steep and gains height quickly with widening views as you climb, both behind to the curve of Ullswater and right into the deepening shadowy depths of Grisedale and across to the bulk of Birkhouse Moor and Striding Edge.

The view back down to Ullswater from the shoulder of St Sunday Crag

Higher up the angle eases and the path heads for the shoulder of Birks, reaching the ridge midway between Birks and St Sunday Crag. Continue the rise directly up the broad ridge to the summit of St Sunday Crag.

St Sunday Crag is superb for views down into Grisedale and across to the edges of Helvellyn, Nethermost Pike and Dollywaggon Pike, as well as across Deepdale to the northern cliffs of Fairfield and Hart Crag.

The path crosses the broad summit dome in a southwest direction making the short descent to Deepdale Hause, where the paths from Grisedale and Deepdale meet. The continuation to Fairfield is up a broken rocky ridge, a steadying hand needed here and there as you cross the rocky summit of Cofa Pike. It is a short climb now to the broad, bulky summit of Fairfield.

Fairfield sits at the junction of several ridges and provides the high-point of both this round and the more famous Fairfield Horseshoe. Its broad summit plateau dominates the valley heads of both Rydal Beck and Deepdale and gives grand views of virtually every fell in the Lake

District. The summit itself is close to the northern crags and is marked by a modest stone wind shelter.

To continue, head southeast for a few hundred metres, then pick up the broad path which swings east, then southeast along the broad ridge, soon with views right into Rydal. There is a short descent into the gap of Link Hause before the rise to Hart Crag, the third major summit of the day.

Like Fairfield, Hart Crag is a broad, stony summit and it is not always easy to decide on the highest point (just to the right of the main path). The main ridge path continues southeast to Dove Crag, but our way heads northeast aiming for the long finger-like edge of Hartsop Above How. In clear conditions you will be able to see the lower section of the ridge below and you should have no problem locating it, but things will be more tricky in poor visibility. Head northeast (on a bearing of approx. 60 degrees) from the summit to locate the cairned path which descends through steep rocky ground. Once over this, the long central section of the ridge is straightforward and enjoyable.

Lower down a wall follows the ridge crest. Stay within sight of this on the right until you are almost at the bottom of the ridge approaching woods ahead. The path trends left away from the wall here to reach a small gate in the fence. Go through the gate and walk down through woods to go through a second gate into a large field. Go ahead across the field to a farm track and follow this rightwards to the road at Deepdale Bridge. Turn left along the road and return past the Youth Hostel to Patterdale to complete the route.

Looking back to Fairfield from Hartsop Above How

The long edge of Rough Crag and High Street from Haweswater

14. *High Street from Haweswater*

Outline: *A long but not too demanding walk up a shapely, distinctive ridge with fine views and a steep final climb to High Street. There are two options for a return—straightforward walking around Riggindale and over Kidsty Pike, or by a slightly tougher alternative along the skyline above Blea Water and Small Water.*

Distance: *11.5km/7 miles.*

Height gained: *850m/2,800ft.*

Summits: *High Street, Mardale Ill Bell, Harter Fell for the southern circuit. High Street, Rampsgill Head, Kidsty Pike for the northern circuit.*

Starting point: *Car park at the head of Haweswater.*
Grid ref: NY 469 107.

THINK OF HIGH STREET and no vivid mountain image comes to mind as it does with the mention of Blencathra, Skiddaw or the Langdale Pikes. High Street is hidden amongst the broad, high moors of the northeastern fells—a high Pennine-like plateauland, deeply-cut by long glacial valleys but with no memorable skylines. Yet up close, High Street can provide fine mountain drama, with narrow ridges, high crags and deep mountain lakes—like a softer version of Helvellyn.

Without a doubt, the finest approach to High Street is along the narrow edge of Rough Crag, the dramatic fall into Riggindale on one side and the spectacular amphitheatre containing Blea Water on the other. From the summit you have a choice of descents. Your decision will probably depend on whether or not you have already walked the Kentmere Horseshoe, in which case the northern loop over Kidsty Pike will save any duplication.

The route: Go through the gate at the end of the little car park and follow the broad path ahead. This is part of an old bridleway over the hills south to Longsleddale and is still classified for vehicles although

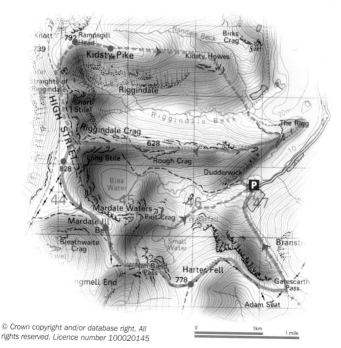

0   1km
        1 mile

High Street and Blea Water from Mardale Ill Bell

you would have to be very brave to drive this route. In 100m or so, at a path junction, turn right at the corner of the wall and follow the path over two footbridges. Bear right after the second bridge and soon you will be walking above the lake towards the wooded headland known as 'The Rigg'. As you approach the woods the path bears left up to the crest of the ridge. Go through a gap in the wall and bear left almost immediately to start the long ascent of the Rough Crag ridge.

There are grand views down the length of Haweswater as well as down into Riggindale and across to the shapely summit of Kidsty Pike, one of the options for the return leg.

The path is easy and ascends with the wall on the left past occasional birch trees until it passes through a gap in the wall. The path is much steeper now and climbs up to gain the crest again by the wall. Once you are over this section the walking is much easier and you can cruise along and enjoy the widening views on both sides.

To the left you will see the two tarns of Small Water and Blea Water in their dark glacial valleys. Blea Water's claim to fame is its depth—at 63m/207 feet, it is the deepest tarn in the Lake District by a long way and of the larger valley lakes is only exceeded by Wast Water and Windermere.

A small cairn marks the summit of Rough Crag after which the ridge drops to a small grassy saddle known as Caspel Gate where there is a small pool. Ahead the ridge steepens again for the final 200m climb up Long Stile Edge to the summit. The ridge is steep and rough but there is no difficulty and you are soon on the summit, its broad, grassy plateau coming as an anticlimax after the shapely ridge of the ascent.

The highest point lies 300m to the southwest marked by an Ordnance Survey triangulation pillar, but the views are better from here where you can look back down the ridge to Haweswater and into the shadowy depths of Blea Water over 300m below. High Street takes its name from the Roman road which passed over its summit linking the forts at Ambleside (Galava) and Brougham (Brocavvm) near Penrith. On some older maps you will notice the fell's alternative name 'Racecourse Hill'. This originates from the late nineteenth and early twentieth centuries when the broad, flat summit was used for horse racing as part of annual Mardale Shepherd's Meet.

There are two main options for a return to Haweswater. You can head north on the good path along the ridge beside the wall and across the head of Riggindale, then bear northeast where the path forks to

On the summit of Rough Crag looking to High Street

the broad bulky summit of Rampsgill Head. Summit collectors will not be able to miss the short out-and-back walk to High Raise, before continuing to the fine little summit of Kidsty Pike with its superb views into Riggindale and across to Rough Crag and High Street. From Kidsty Pike a good path descends almost due east for 1.5km/1 mile before heading down through the broken rocks of Kidsty Howes. Lower down, just above the lake, you pass close to Randale Beck on the left before bearing right to cross the stone bridge over Riggindale Beck. Follow the well-used footpath back beside the woods of The Rigg to finish the walk.

Alternatively, from High Street you can head south beside the wall to pick up the path which forks left to Mardale III Bell—a summit which slips by hardly noticed—then descends to the Nan Bield Pass where there is a small but distinctive square stone wind shelter. From there the ridge rises to Harter Fell and a continuation can be made to Gatescarth Pass.

To shorten the walk, you can descend from the Nan Bield Pass via Small Water. For this option take the path left (north) from the pass which weaves down to pass to the left of the lake. The path crosses the outflow stream at the point where it leaves the lake, then bears left down the valley beside the stream on the left. Lower down the path bears away from the stream to pass through a wall and continues down to the path junction just before the car park.

For the continuation over Harter Fell, make the rise from the Nan Bield Pass to Harter Fell, a straightforward climb of about 150m in just under 1km/¾ mile. The summit is marked by a distinctive cairn composed of stones and pieces of old rusting metal fence posts. Take care not to follow the path by the fence which heads south (right) to the distant Kentmere Pike, instead, follow the fence northeast (leftwards as you approach the summit) along the rounded ridge top. At the corner of the fence turn right and follow the path down to join the unsurfaced lane which crosses the pass (Gatescarth Pass). Turn left and follow the track back to the car park to finish the walk.

The South

Pike o' Stickle rising above Mickleden

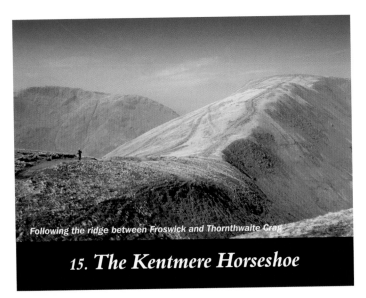

Following the ridge between Froswick and Thornthwaite Crag

15. The Kentmere Horseshoe

Outline: *Easy walking from Kentmere village on a good bridleway leads onto the broad ridge. A steeper rise to the first summit is followed by superb ridge walking on good paths with extensive views. The second half of the horseshoe is less interesting and can be left out if needed, but this would change the character of the walk. The final few miles are easy with a gradual descent of a broad gentle ridge with farm tracks back to Kentmere.*

Distance: *21km/13 miles.*

Height gained: *1,210m/3,910ft.*

Summits: *Yoke, Ill Bell, Froswick, Thornthwaite Crag, High Street, Mardale Ill Bell, Harter Fell, Kentmere Pike, Shipman Knotts.*

Starting point: *There is very limited parking in Kentmere village so an early arrival is essential. A handful of cars can be parked by the institute adjacent to the church. Begin the walk by the church. Grid ref: NY 457 041.*

THIS ROUTE IS A RIDGE WALKER'S DREAM. Once the main ridge is gained most of the work is done and you can enjoy miles of elevated walking on good paths with minimal effort between summits and stunning views west towards Helvellyn and St Sunday Crag, and southwest to the long finger of Windermere. Although quite a long circuit, there is minimal rise and fall between each summit and with good paths under foot the miles slip by surprisingly easily. The second half of the horseshoe can be left out with an easier return along the valley from the Nan Bield Pass if needed.

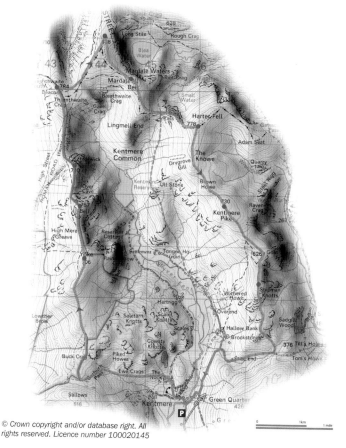

Ill Bell from Yoke

The route: From the church follow the lane away from the village and take the first lane on the left. In about 150m, and immediately after the house 'Green Head' on the right, turn right onto the path signed for 'Garburn Pass'. The path rises easily as a wide cobbled track (an old lane over the fells to Troutbeck), passing a huge boulder in the field on the left known as 'Badger Rock', a well known local landmark.

Follow the track up onto the rounded crest of the ridge where you pass through a gate almost at the highest point. In 100m or so, turn right on a grass path which heads directly across the boggy, sloping moors roughly parallel to the wall away to the right. Further on, the path runs close by the wall and you meet a broad surfaced path which continues the climb to the first summit of the day—Yoke.

This summit is a broad grassy plateau marked by a single cairn, but it gives you your first proper views out over the peaks of central and eastern Lakeland and back to the long finger of Windermere. This is also the first view of the ridge ahead, dominated by the fine shapely summit of Ill Bell.

The well-made path continues along the narrowing ridge crest to the summit of Ill Bell with its collection of stone cairns and view down to the Kentmere Reservoir.

Almost the entire walk can now be seen—the continuation to Froswick and Thornthwaite Crag, and High Street at the head of the Kentmere valley, and the second half of the ridge beyond the Nan Bield Pass over Harter Fell and Kentmere Pike.

The path continues over the less interesting summit of Froswick and along the connecting ridge to Thornthwaite Crag where the line of the old Roman road reaches the ridge from Troutbeck. Thornthwaite Crag is an expansive summit with a tall stone cairn bult into the corner of the stone wall which crosses the ridge here. Like Ill Bell it would be hard to mistake this top even in the poorest visibility. In clear weather its central location gives it grand views west to Helvellyn, St Sunday Crag and Dove Crag, and north down to Ullswater. South, the view includes the Ill Bell and Froswick rising above the Kentmere valley.

From Thornthwaite Crag the path curves east, then north with views down to Hayeswater. The main path is approximately on the line of the Roman road here and is probably wide enough to accommodate a marching army. As you approach High Street, break away right to reach the summit marked by an Ordnance Survey triangulation pillar.

Looking back along the ridge to Froswick and Ill Bell from Thornthwaite Crag

Views from the summit are restricted by the wide flat expanse of grass, but a short walk east to the lip of Blea Water Crag gives a grand view down into the head of Mardale with both Blea Water and Haweswater visible below.

Bear right now along the edge of the broken cliffs which fall to Blea Water to the next top—Mardale Ill Bell—an indistinct rise on the broad moors but with excellent views left to the northern slopes of High Street rising above Blea Water—the deepest tarn in the Lake District at 63m/207 feet. A little further on the path drops to Nan Bield Pass, an ancient route over the fells marked by a square stone wind shelter.

(The walk could be cut short here if needed by following the zig-zaging path right. This heads across the slopes of Harter Fell above the Kentmere Reservoir, then along the valley bottom to join the lane end near the farms of Hallow Bank and Brockstones. Follow the lane back to Kentmere.)

The climb out of the Nan Bield Pass to the broad summit of Harter Fell is soon over and tired legs will be grateful for the easy gradients from now on. The highest point is marked by a cairn and close by is a fence which divides the broad ridge. Follow the path right beside the fence for almost 2km/1¼ miles, the slight fall and rise to Kentmere Pike barely noticed.

From Kentmere Pike the path continues beside the wall southeast for just over 1km/¾ mile to cross a ladder stile in a crossing wall. Shipman Knotts, little more than a slight rise on the ridge, marks the final summit of the day. From here the path continues south beside the wall to join the old track linking Kentmere with Longsleddale. Turn right and follow the track down to the tarmac lane in the Kentmere valley. Turn left along the lane for about 1km/¾ mile and take the first lane on the right. Follow this down to the T junction and turn right to return to the church to complete the route.

The Fairfield Horseshoe from Loughrigg Fell

16. The Fairfield Horseshoe

Outline: *A long high-level ridge walk over several summits with superb views in all directions. After an initially steep climb to gain the ridge, moderate, elevated ridge walking follows the skyline of the Rydal Beck valley. Paths are generally good with some boggy sections. There are also sections around the summits of Fairfield and Hart Crag which need care in poor visibility.*

Distance: *17km/10½ miles.*

Height gained: *1,100m/3,630ft.*

Summits: *Nab Scar, Heron Pike, Great Rigg, Fairfield, Hart Crag, Dove Crag, High Pike, Low Pike.*

Starting point: *The hamlet of Rydal where there is a small car park over the little stone bridge on the left immediately before Rydal (approaching from Ambleside). Turn right immediately after the bridge and the car park is on the left. Alternatively, cars are sometimes parked in the lane by Rydal Mount.*
Grid ref: NY 364 060.

THE FAIRFIELD HORSESHOE is one of the best known ridge walks in the Lake District and as such is on every fell walker's 'must do' list. Its fame and popularity is well deserved, eight summits linked by a graceful undulating ridge with not too much height loss between and wide views in every direction. Satisfaction guaranteed.

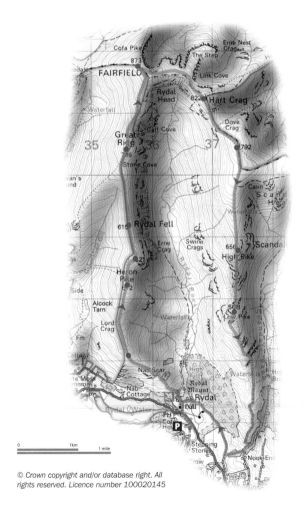

A view along the ridge to Heron Pike, Great Rigg, Fairfiled and Hart Crag

The route: From the little car park follow lane back over the bridge to the main road and turn left. In about 250m, cross the road and turn right up the lane to Rydal Hall immediately before the church. Walk up the lane passing the hall on the right and 'Rydal Mount and Gardens' on the left. Ignore the first signed footpath on the left (Coffin Path) continuing to the end of the surfaced road where there are two stone houses. Bear left past the second house and through a kissing gate to join a footpath enclosed between widely spaced stone walls. This path rises steeply, soon as a pitched path which zig-zags up to reach the first summit of the day, Nab Scar, where the angle eases.

Good views open out from here down to Rydal Water and to the south where Windermere is now visible beyond Ambleside. It is not easy to decide on the highest point as Nab Scar is more of a ridge end than a true summit. You will no doubt find the gentle contours ahead something of a relief after the steep ascent so far.

The well-defined path now heads along the broad undulating ridge with a more gentle rise to Heron Pike. This is a much better summit with a grand view of the entire route ahead—from Great Rigg, over Fairfield and Dove Crag with the return leg over High Pike and Low Pike.

The view to Ambleside and Windermere from Nab Scar

Heron Pike has two summits, the northern top being the higher by a few metres and a further 500m along the ridge above Erne Crag, almost the only crag to scar this western side of the Rydal Beck valley.

The ridge ahead is looking more appealing all the time and with just 250m of ascent to achieve in over 3km/2 miles, most of the tough work is behind you. Here you can fully appreciate the wild impressive valley around which this walk passes—over 5km/3 miles long and 300m deep it is greatly foreshortened when viewed from Ambleside or Rydal Park.

The route along the ridge continues almost due north and virtually level for the next 2km1¼ miles allowing you to relax and enjoy the impressive surroundings and the widening views ahead to Great Rigg and Fairfield, and around the great arc of fells enclosing Rydal Beck forming the second half of the walk. Helvellyn should now be visible along with Dollywaggon Pike and Seat Sandal. West across the hidden pass of Dunmail Raise are stacked nearly all the central and southern fells, from the High Raise past Bowfell and Crinkle Crags to the Coniston Fells.

A short steeper climb of almost 100m brings you to Great Rigg, the final top before the high point of the day—Fairfield itself. Great Rigg is perhaps the most shapely summit on the whole round and is particularly impressive from the eastern arm of the horseshoe rising 400m above the head of the valley. The view has continued to improve all the way along the ridge adding more summits to the growing list.

A little over 1km/¾ miles separates Great Rigg from Fairfield, again the way is obvious but becomes less so as you approach the wide, featureless summit plateau, particularly in poor visibility. A line of small ruined cairns marks the final few metres to the modest stone wind shelters.

At 873m/2,864ft, Fairfield is the highest point on the round as well as its mid point. From here the ridge curves east, then southeast over Hart Crag and Dove Crag, fells better known from their more impressive northerly approaches. Although Fairfield remains the centre piece of the Fairfield Horseshoe throughout the walk, the mountain's southern slopes are not it's most impressive. To see this fell at its best you must view it from the north where it rises at the head of Deepdale, its broad, bald summit dominating a wall of dark crags over 1km/¾ mile wide. With these crags invisible from above, those visiting its summit on the Fairfield Horseshoe will most likely remember it for the extensive views which now take in just about every summit of note in Lakeland.

Take care to locate the correct path from Fairfield to Hart Crag, especially in poor visibility as the featureless plateau looks much the same in every direction. Remember that the summit lies a little to the

Looking down the ridge to High Pike

north, so you will need to head southeast for a few hundred metres to avoid the broken crags which fall into Cawk Cove (particularly dangerous in icy conditions) before picking up the path which heads almost due east, then southeast. Make a short descent into the gap of Link Hause before continuing to Hart Crag, the fifth summit of the day.

Hart Crag is shattered and stony and the footpath skirts the highest point a few metres to the north. Again this is confusing terrain in poor visibility. Southeast from Hart Crag the ridge drops again before a short rise to the broad gentler dome of Dove Crag. Due south the route continues beside the ruined remains of an old stone wall. Take care here not to follow a path which breaks east to Little Hart Crag.

The ridge is more plateau-like now, the crest marked by the old wall all the way to High Pike. The main feature of this section are the views west across the Rydal Beck valley to the shapely summit of Great Rigg, the distant views beyond to the Coniston and Langdale fells and the sweeping narrow edge ascended earlier in the walk. The path continues beside the wall as it snakes all the way down to Low Pike, an excellent little summit and just about the only feature on the long descent from Dove Crag towards Ambleside.

The wall remains your guide as you continue the descent, England's largest lake rolled out ahead. Lower down the main path swings left below the walled ridge crest, but an alternative path follows the wall to rejoin the main route immediately before a large gateway in a crossing wall. After the gateway a good path continues the descent to cross Scandale Beck at Low Sweden Bridge. Immediately before the bridge there is a permissive path on the right where the main path bends sharp left. Follow this path down beside the beck to join the footpath through Rydal Park. Turn right and follow the track to Rydal Hall. *(Continuing along the track over Low Sweden Bridge will take you to Ambleside.)*

As you approach Rydal Hall and gardens bear right as signed and follow the road over the bridge and past Rydal Hall to reach the lane. Turn left down the lane and retrace the outward route to complete the walk.

Pike o' Stickle, Loft Crag and Harrison Stickle from Blea Tarn

17. *The Langdale Pikes*

Outline: *A steep climb from the valley gets you onto the tops quickly. This is followed by much easier walking over high moorland where the closely grouped summits of the Langdale Pikes can be ticked off with ease. The descent is steep and rocky by way of Stickle Tarn and Stickle Ghyll.*

Distance: *8.5km/5¼ miles.*

Height gained: *820m/2,690ft.*

Summits: *Loft Crag, Pike o' Stickle, Harrison Stickle, Pavey Ark (Thunacar Knott optional).*

Starting point: *National Trust car park beside the 'Sticklebarn Tavern' and WC in the Great Langdale. Grid ref: NY 295 064.*

THE LANGDALE PIKES demonstrate to perfection that height is not everything. They completely dominate a valley noted for its rugged summits, holding their own against fells which stand head and shoulders above them. Only when there is snow on the ground are you fully aware that the neighbouring fells are so much higher.

This is a relatively short round which gets you high quickly and catches all the main tops, as well as visiting Stickle Tarn in its impressive setting below the huge southern face of Pavey Ark.

The route: From the roofed interpretation sign beside the toilets in the corner of the car park, follow the footpath left between the wall and fence. Go through a gate, pass between stone walls into a small field and follow the path up the field to the top left-hand corner ignoring a path on the right. The footpath forks here—bear left and follow the rising path to go through a kissing gate. Where the path forks again bear right by a wall. Soon, cross the gill on the left (Dungeon Ghyll) and follow the pitched path which rises more steeply now giving increasingly spectacular views down into Langdale and across the valley to the distinctive little summit of Side Pike.

The angle eases to give a brief respite on the plateau above Mark Gate and below the final climb to Loft Crag. The high point of the

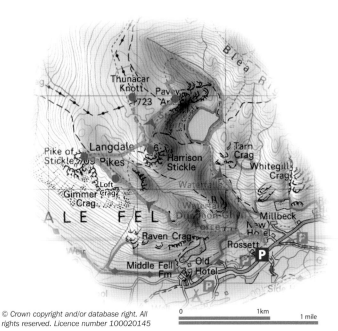

Pike o' Stickle and Loft Crag from the valley

day—Harrison Stickle—can now be seen up to the right. Continue up the final steep slopes to arrive on the ridge.

It comes as a surprise after the steep 500m climb from the valley to find yourself not on the crest of a high ridge, but the lip of flat rolling moorland, but the pointed rocky summit of Loft Crag, a little way to the left, compensates. Head left on the path to Loft Crag, the first summit of the day. There are good views ahead to the striking outline of Pike o' Stickle, its southern face falling steeply into Mickleden and across the valley to the bulky summit of Bowfell.

Beyond Loft Crag the continuation to Pike o' Stickle is a delight after the tough climb from the valley. You can stride out effortlessly and take in the stunning surroundings. The final rise to Pike o' Stickle involves a short section of straightforward but unavoidable scrambling, once over this, you can enjoy the superb setting of one of Lakeland's finest summits.

Make your way back down the scramble to the footpath and bear left on a curving line across the broad, shallow hollow of Harrison

Combe, heading north first, then swing east up to the broad ridge line midway between Harrison Stickle and Thunacar Knott to join the broad footpath between the two. *Thunacar Knott can be included easily from here by a short out-and-back detour to the left.* Follow the footpath right now meandering around rocky knolls and boggy hollows to reach the summit of Harrison Stickle.

From here you get your first view of Pavey Ark—the final summit of the day—along with Stickle Tarn lying at the foot of the huge south face of the mountain. You can also enjoy the superb view along Langdale and out to Windermere.

A cairned footpath heads north along the edge of the steep slopes which sweep down to Stickle Tarn. This path is easily lost, but you will find it again as you continue and no footpath is really needed here anyway. The summit of Pavey Ark lies on the very edge of the cliffs directly above the tarn so take care in poor visibility.

It is important to locate the correct footpath for the descent to avoid going too far to the right near the cliff edge. There is an intermittent stone wall near the summit—the well-worn, cairned footpath is beyond this and very obvious, so if you have any doubts you haven't gone far enough. The footpath is rough, rocky and steep and descends within a stone's throw of the cliffs to the right although they remain out of sight.

Harrison Stickle and Loft Crag from Pike o' Stickle

On the summit of Pike o' Stickle

At the bottom of the steep slope the path crosses the beck then follows the shore of the lake to the outflow by the small dam. It is worth a brief halt here to take in the impressive surroundings and prepare yourself for the steep descent beside Stickle Ghyll.

Paths descend on either side of the stream but the main path follows the right-hand bank. This begins the descent immediately adjacent to the stream and is rough and rocky at first, but soon becomes much easier as you reach the pitching. About 100m below the lake the path forks where there are small slabby cliffs on the far side. Bear left and cross the stream by the large stepping stones. The path follows the left-hand bank now.

There is a narrower and steeper path which descends all the way from the tarn on the left-hand side of the stream, but this is much steeper and harder on tired knees. Both paths converge immediately before a group of small pines. A little lower down, bear right over a stile and shortly cross a footbridge over the stream. The path is straightforward now and follows the stream back to the car park to complete the route.

Crinkle Crags and Bowfell from the summit of Pike o' Blisco

18. Pike o' Blisco & Crinkle Crags from Great Langdale

Outline: *A steep climb out of the lower valley followed by open fell sides leads to Pike o' Blisco with is superb views of the route ahead. This is followed by a rough descent to Red Tarn, then easy walking up to the ridge where you negotiate the first of the 'crinkles'. From here the ridge walking is as good as anything in the Lake District. Occasional easy scrambling takes you over several sub summits until you are faced with the famous 'Bad Step' in the final rise to the highest top. If you like to get your hands on the rock this will be over too soon, if not you can easily avoid it. Return to the valley is by the long, gentle eastern ridge of Bowfell known as The Band.*

Distance: *12km/7½miles.*

Height gained: *1,050m/3,500ft.*

Summits: *Pike o' Blisco, Crinkle Crags (Bowfell optional).*

Start: *The National Park car park beside the 'Old Dungeon Ghyll Hotel' near the head of Great Langdale. Grid ref: NY 285 060.*

CRINKLE CRAGS SUFFERS SLIGHTLY from its closeness to both Bow-fell—whose imposing mass dominates the head of the valley, and the Langdale Pikes which form one of the most attractive centrepieces to any valley in the region. But tucked away at the head of the wild Ox-endale, Crinkle Crags' undulating rocky ridge provides one of the most enjoyable high-level walks in the Lake District—a swithchback rocky ridge with occasional easy scrambling and wide views.

This route begins with a traverse of the adjacent Pike o' Blisco giving superb views of the route ahead, but this can easily be by-passed and left for another day if you prefer.

The route: Turn left out of the car park, cross the bridge and turn right along the lane. At the T Junction turn left and follow the lane over the bridge near the campsite on the left. Almost immediately, take the signed path on the left into the campsite. In about 100m bear right over a footbridge and follow the footpath ahead which soon rises steeply up the open fell side. Higher up a stile over the wall leads onto the road at the summit of Blea Tarn Pass.

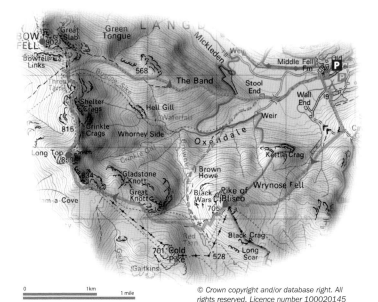

The view to Crinkle Crags main summit with Gunson Knott to the right separated by the scree gully of Mickle Door (the distant summit of Bowfell is just visible)

Cross the road (don't cross the cattle grid) and bear half-right onto the contouring footpath opposite. This is faint at first but becomes better established where it joins the pitched path coming up from the lower valley to the right by the stream. The pitched path rises steeply and directly up beside the stream.

There are superb views right to the famous Langdale Pikes throughout much of ascent to Pike o' Blisco.

The angles eases on the high shoulder of the fell and the path swings rightwards up the final broken, rocky slopes where views open out southwards to the Coniston Fells.

Pike o' Blisco is surprisingly rocky for a fell of such modest altitude and has two summits, the highest being the westernmost and marked by a large stone cairn. There are superb views from here of the route ahead—the multi-topped Crinkle Crags, Bowfell looking imposing at the head of Oxendale and the long blunt arm of The Band used as the descent route.

Take the path which weaves southwest steeply down the rocky slopes to Red Tarn which occupies the pass between Pike o' Blisco and Cold Pike.

(To reach Red Tarn without making the ascent of Pike o' Blisco, walk left out of the car park by the 'Old Dungeon Ghyll Hotel', cross the bridge and turn right. At the T junction by the post box, go through the gate ahead and take the farm access road which heads across the flat valley floor and over Oxendale Beck to Stool End Farm. Pass through the farmyard and out of the large gate to the left of the farmhouse. Follow the farm track ahead ignoring the path which breaks right and go through the gate. Follow the track beside the rocky Oxendale Beck and at stone sheep pens take the signed path left. Go through the gates and continue beside the beck to the footbridge. Cross the bridge and bear right on the footpath. This soon swings leftwards to rise as a steep but clear pitched path.

Higher up the angle eases as the path climbs beside Browney Gill down to the right. At the top of the pass and before the tarn you reach a T junction with the path running between Pike o' Blisco and Crinkle Crags. Turn right for Crinkle Crags.)

Looking back to Pike o' Blisco from Crinkle Crags over a 'sea' of fog

From the pass at Red Tarn the path climbs west up onto the broad grassy plateau between Great Knott and Cold Pike (both out-and-back detours if you are collecting summits). The broad well-used path continues ahead, soon with the pointed tops of Crinkle Crags visible on the skyline.

The first of Crinkle Crag's summits is a short easy scramble and allows you your first proper view of the ridge ahead. Continue along the ridge making short descents and rises with occasional easy scrambling here and there. Immediately before the final rise to the highest top, you reach the famous 'Bad Step'. Despite being much harder than anything you will have encountered so far, it should present the average agile walker with no problems. The gully above is blocked by two large boulders, but the key is to use the right-hand wall requiring one or two simple moves and you're over it. A short climb over boulders leads to the summit. *(The Bad Step can be avoided by a path on the left.)*

From the summit you can look along the ridge now all the way to Bowfell, an attractive pointed fell from here.

The path continues across the top of Mickle Door, a wide scree gully separating the main summit from Gunson Knott. The path skirts the

Looking along the ridge to Bowfell

Negotiating the 'Bad Step' on the final climb to the summit of Crinkle Crags

latter continuing just below the crest all the way to Three Tarns, the pass immediately before the steep rise to Bowfell.

(Bowfell is an out-and-back walk up the slopes ahead, or, If you have any energy left you could continue over Bowfell to Ore Gap, descend to Angle Tarn and return by the Rossett Gill path through Micklden but this would make a long mountain day.)

Take the path right at Three Tarns. This soon forks—keep left (the right-hand option leads down beside Hell Gill into upper Oxendale and can be used as an alternative) on the path which traverses almost to the crest of the broad ridge with views down into Mickleden and across to Pike o' Stickle.

The path down The Band is straightforward but long and in about 2.5km/1½ miles joins the farm track leading from Oxendale to Stool End Farm. Turn left and go through the farmyard, then follow the farm road across the flat valley floor back to the lane by the 'Old Dungeon Ghyll Hotel' to complete the route.

Bowfell and The Band from the slopes of Pike o' Blisco

19. Bowfell & Esk Pike from Great Langdale

Outline: *The long, laborious climb up The Band is legendary but no where is the ascent particularly steep and views are excellent in clear conditions. Three Tarns pass is a superb spot to catch your breath for the final steep rocky ascent to Bowfell. Level walking across the stony plateau is followed by a short descent to Ore Gap and rise to Esk Pike. Easy walking leads from Esk Pike down to Esk Hause and Angle Tarn to the head of Rossett Gill. A long descent on a pitched path into Mickleden with striking views to Pike o' Stickle and a flat walk along the valley to complete the walk.*

Distance: *14km/8¾ miles.*

Height gained: *1,000m/3,300ft.*

Summits: *Bowfell, Esk Pike, Rossett Pike.*

Start: *The National Park car park beside the 'Old Dungeon Ghyll Hotel' near the head of Great Langdale. Grid ref: NY 285 060.*

THE FIRST-TIME VISITOR TO LANGDALE will most likely be drawn to the striking outlines of the Langdale Pikes. They dominate much of the lower valley with their pointed, rocky summits and fist-like buttresses and appear to be higher, or at least just as high as the less remarkable summits at the head of the valley. But this is just an illusion, Bowfell presides over Langdale like a great throne, its height and bulk only apparent on closer inspection.

This route approaches Bowfell by the long, chunky arm known as The Band—a deceptively long, but easy ridge which carries walkers from valley floor to the high shoulder of the mountain. A high-level ridge walk then leads over Bowfell and Esk Pike. Save this walk for a day of good visibility as the summits of both Bowfell and Esk Pike can be bewildering in misty conditions.

The route: Walk left out of the car park, cross over the bridge and turn right. At the T junction by the post box, go through the gate ahead and follow the farm access road which heads across the flat valley floor and over Oxendale Beck to Stool End Farm. Pass through the farmyard and out of the large gate to the left of the farmhouse. Follow the broad rocky

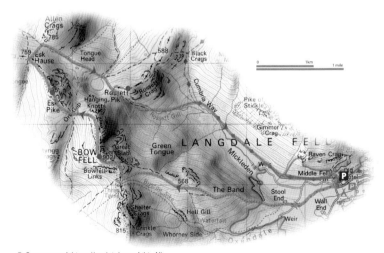

farm track ahead by the wall, but look for the path which soon breaks away right (in about 200m) to begin the long climb up The Band, the mountain's long, blunt, eastern arm.

The path heads up to a narrow gate in the upper wall by the Harmer memorial. Go through the gate and continue the climb for 2.5km/1½ miles, mainly on the southern side of the broad ridge crest. In the central section the gradient eases before the final steeper rise to the pass at Three Tarns (it is worth the detour right above Ealing Crag for the view down into Mickleden before you reach the top of the ridge).

If you are confident on steep ground the variation know as the 'Climber's Traverse' offers a more adventurous route to the summit. This branches right from the shoulder (grid ref: 253 063) and cuts across the northeast face of the mountain below Flat Crags to reach a point with impressive views ahead to Bowfell Buttress. Here the path swings up left over rocky ground, soon beside Great Slab, to reach the summit. This route is exposed in places so avoid it if you are unsure of your ability over such terrain or in icy conditions.

Three Tarns is named after the small pools which make excellent foregrounds for views across the wilds of Eskdale to the Scafell group and Bowfell. Bowfell looks quite imposing from here, its pointed summit rising above the line of crags known as Bowfell Links.

The impressive view of Bowfell from Three Tarns

Great Slab near the summit of Bowfell with the Langdale Pikes in the distance

You meet the well-used path which runs between Crinkle Crags and Bowfell just before the tarns. Turn right and follow the rocky path, rising steeply through a break in the southern cliffs to reach the flat summit plateau. The highest point is obvious enough in clear weather rising to a fine point. In poor visibility this area can be confusing but the path is cairned.

If you didn't go for the 'Climber's Traverse' option on the way up it is worth walking over to the eastern edge of the summit plateau in clear weather for the view of the famous Great Slab set against the distant Langdale Pikes. This view was immortalised by the late Alfred Wainwright in his pictorial guide to Bowfell.

From Bowfell head north on the cairned path which skirts the northern summit before dropping into Ore Gap—the pass which separates Bowfell from Esk Pike. (*If you want to shorten the walk leaving out Esk Pike a good path descends right from here down to Angle Tarn. As the angle steepens the path bears left to meet the Esk Hause path. Make sure you keep to the path in poor visibility as there are cliffs below.*)

From Ore Gap a moderate rise up the final rocky slopes leads to the summit of Esk Pike. Being almost at the centre of the Lakeland fells the view is extensive with all but the far eastern fells visible.

From Esk Pike the path descends northwest to Esk Hause. Ahead, the broad ridge rises to Great End, then swings south to Scafell Pike. Bear right from Esk Hause and descend to another broad saddle immediately before the rise to Allen Crags where there is a cross-shaped wind shelter (a good land mark in poor visibility). Head right from here on the footpath which descends across the head of Langstrath—the long empty valley on the left—and below the broken northern crags of Esk Pike to Angle Tarn.

Cross the outflow stream from the tarn by the stepping stones and take the rising footpath to the head of Rossett Gill, immediately below Rossett Pike. This small summit is ascended mainly on account of its inclusion in the lists of both the Wainwrights and the Nuttalls 2,000ft summits, but it is also superb for views down Mickleden and across to the striking rock pillar of Pike o' Stickle.

Return to the top of Rossett Gill and take the long descent path left. The path, which is now pitched, zig-zags rightwards across the lower slopes of Bowfell and proves to be much longer than it initially looks.

The strange hummocks in the bottom of the valley are glacial moraines deposited by a small glacier or snowfield which formed on this side of Bowfell during a late glacial period. They are composed of rocks and soil transported by the glacier and mark the lower limit of the ice.

In the bottom of the valley, cross the footbridge and take the well-used path back to the 'Old Dungeon Ghyll Hotel' to complete the route.

Great Carrs from Swirl How with the central fells in the distance

20. *The Coniston Fells*

Outline: *The Walna Scar Road leads with minimal effort almost to the first summit, Brown Pike. Once on the ridge the walking is easy on good paths taking in the summits of Dow Crag and the Old Man of Coniston. Easy walking along the broad ridge allows you to tick off Brim Fell, Swirl How, Great Carrs and Grey Friar with minimal effort. Return is made by Levers Water using good footpaths and mining roads.*

Distance: *18km/11¼ miles.*

Height gained: *1,330m/4,360ft.*

Summits: *Dow Crag, Old Man of Coniston, Brim Fell, Swirl How, Great Carrs, Grey Friar.*

Starting point: *The usual starting point for this round is the head of the Walna Scar road where there is free parking on common land. Grid ref: SD 288 970. This is reached by the very steep lane out of Coniston which gets busy in the summer. An alternative start is from the centre of Coniston where there is a large pay and display car park but this requires a longer walk up the lane.*

THE CONISTON FELLS are some of the most popular summits in the Lake District making it almost impossible to avoid the crowds here. In clear conditions, however, it is easy to see why—they offer some of the finest views in Lakeland, particularly north to the high central fells headed by the Scafell group and south out over the green fingers of the south Lakeland peninsulas. The central section of the route along the broad, almost level ridge between the Old Man of Coniston and Swirl How offers some of the most enjoyable walking imaginable—easy underfoot with unrivalled views.

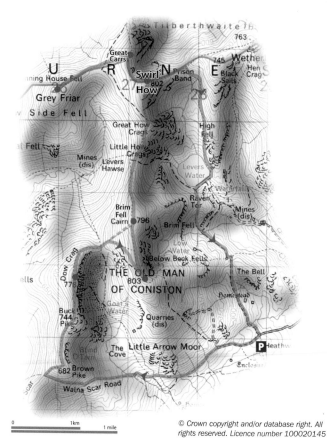

Looking along the ridge from Brown Pike to Buck Pike

The town of Coniston can be used as the starting point but it is both famous and popular so it will be busy throughout the summer months. The usual start is from the high car park on the Walna Scar Road at the end of a very steep lane out of Coniston. To reach this from the car park in the centre of Coniston, turn left past the church and cross the bridge. Turn right immediately and walk up the lane passing the 'Sun Inn'. At the T junction turn right and where the lane bends sharp left take the lane ahead, signed 'Walna Scar'. This rises steeply to a parking area where the tarmac ends.

The route: From the parking area continue ahead along the gently rising track (just about good enough for 4x4 cars for much of its length) to its high point on the saddle separating Brown Pike from Walna Scar where a wide view to the Scafell group opens out (3km/1¾ miles).

Take the good footpath right from here to the summit of Brown Pike. This gives the first glimpse of the route ahead over Buck Pike and Dow Crag to the rounded bulk of the Old Man of Coniston and with much of the steep ascent behind you, you can cruise along the ridge taking in the superb setting with wide views in all directions. Most impressive is the view ahead to the high central fells gathered around Scafell and Scafell Pike, but in clear conditions much of the southwest Lakeland coast is also visible across Morecambe Bay to the distant Yorkshire Dales on the skyline.

Follow the path along the ridge over the intermediate top of Buck Pike and on to the rocky summit of Dow Crag. As you make the final scramble to the summit you will catch the occasional glimpse of Goat's Water tucked tight under the east face of the mountain several hundred metres below. This exposure, along with the final few metres composed purely of rock gives Dow Crag the feeling of a true mountain. Something not experienced on the rest of the walk.

The path continues north making a modest descent to the little pass known as Goat's Hawse. The path forks here. Ignore the tempting left fork (unless you want to leave out the Old Man of Coniston) taking the short, steep diagonal path rightwards instead.

The Old Man of Coniston is the most popular summit in the group, most making the steep ascent via the mining path from Low Water. Like Dow Crag, the panorama from here is superb, the main difference being the latter's impressive east face seen out to the west and backed by the distant Isle of Man.

Following the path from Brim Fell to Levers Hawse and Swirl How

The often crowded summit of Coniston Old Man with Coniston and Coniston Water below

Head north now along the broad whale back ridge over Brim Fell and across the pass of Levers Hawse where the ridge narrows before the climb to Little How Crag. It is worth a brief pause here for the view back along the ridge to the shapely Dow Crag with Seathwaite Tarn down to the right, before the rise to Swirl How.

Swirl How once enjoyed the status of being the highest point in the old county of Lancashire (pre 1974 reorganisation). The view is dominated by the high central fells to the north—Scafell, Scafell Pike, Great End, Esk Pike, Bowfell, Crinkle Crags and the Langdale Pikes—seen against a foreground of the curving edge of Great Carrs. The wreckage which can be seen at the foot of the cliffs to the north and on the ridge out to Great Carrs is that of a World War II bomber which hit the ridge in 1944.

Both Great Carrs and Grey Friar are straightforward out-and-back walks, the latter adding about 2km/1¼ miles with 100m height loss.

From Swirl How head due east down the curiously named Prison Band, a grand name for a rather ordinary ridge. At the pass before the rise to Black Sail and Wetherlam, turn right on the good path which heads easily down towards Levers Water.

On a warm summer day this is a grand place to stop and survey the day's walk along the skyline above. There is a large boulder near the dam at the outflow which makes a good foreground for views of the cliffs above and there are several more along the shore which are excellent for stretching out in the sun.

If you started at the high car park on the Walna Scar Road, turn right across the outflow stream from the lake and cross the curving stone dam. Soon after crossing the dam the path swings up left passing fenced mines on the left to reach a small saddle with a view ahead to the Old Man of Coniston. The path ahead drops gently now to eventually cross a small wooden footbridge with a huge boulder ahead. Follow the path leftwards now. This becomes better established after mining remains a little further on. Continue to a path T junction (the path up the northeast ridge of the Old Man), turn left and, ignoring a left fork in a few metres, follow the path which is now almost a 4x4 road as it swings rightwards. The path/track is now easily followed back to the parking area to complete the walk.

To return to Coniston from Levers Water, follow the rough 4x4 road below the lake down past mining buildings and the Youth Hostel. Continue down the access road and at the bridge cross over to the right-hand side of the river. Follow the path to emerge in the lane beside farm buildings. Turn right, then left past the 'Sun Inn' back to Coniston.

Mara Books & Northern Eye Books

www.marabooks.co.uk or www.northerneyebooks.com

Mara Books publish a range of walking books for Cheshire and North Wales and have the following list to date. A complete list of current titles is available on our web site.

North Wales

Mountain and hill walking

Mountain & Hill Walking in Snowdonia

This is a two-volume in-depth guide to every summit of note in the Snowdonia National Park.

Volume 1 – Carneddau, Glyderau, Snowdon and Eifionydd. ISBN 978 1 902512 18 1.

Volume 2 – Moelwynion, Rhinogydd, Arenig, Arans, Dyfi hills and Cadair Idris as well as the Tarrens and Berwyns. ISBN 978 1 902512 22 8.

Snowdonia's best Mountain Walks

ISBN 978 1 902512 19 8. A guide to the classic walks and scrambles on Snowdonia's mountains.

A Pocket guide to Snowdon

ISBN 978 1 902512 16 7. A guide to all Snowdon's recognised routes of ascent, from the six 'Classic Paths' to the many lesser known and less frequented routes.

Leisure walking

Coastal Walks around Anglesey

ISBN 978 1 902512 20 4. A collection of circular walks which explore the varied scenery of Anglesey's beautiful coastline, designated an Area of Outstanding Natural Beauty.

Walking the Isle of Anglesey Coastal Path

ISBN 978 1 902512 15 0. The official guide to the Isle of Anglesey Coastal Path. Includes Ordnance Survey mapping.

Walks on the Lleyn Peninsula
ISBN 978 1 902512 00 6. A collection of circular walks which explore both the wild and beautiful coastline and hills of the Lleyn Peninsula.

Walking in the Conwy Valley
ISBN 978 0 9522409 7 6. A collection of circular walks exploring the varied scenery of this beautiful valley from the Great Orme to Betws-y-coed.

Walking in the Clwydian Range
ISBN 978 1 902512 14 3. A collection of 21 circular walks in the Clwydian Range Area of Outstanding Natural Beauty.

Walking in the Vale of Clwyd & Hiraethog
ISBN 978 0 9559625 3 0. A collection of circular walks exploring the undiscovered country between the Clwydian Range and the Conwy Valley.

Best Walks in North Wales
ISBN 978 0 9553557 3 8. A selection of the best circular walks in North Wales, from the far western tip of Lleyn through the lakes, woods and hills of Snowdonia to the rolling ridge of the Clwydian Range.

The Mountain Men
ISBN 978 1 902512 11 2. This book tells the story of the pioneer rock climbers in Snowdonia in the closing decades of the nineteenth century until the outbreak of World War I.

The Day the Rope Broke
ISBN 978 1 902512 12 9. The story of the first ascent of the Matterhorn by the Victorian mountaineer Edward Whymper and the disaster which followed. Illustrated in colour and black and white.